Too Bad You're Going to Hell

Fly pain free Robbie
02/28/1985 - 03/01/2019

Responses to Readings

Letters From Real People

* * * * *

Hi Terry!

I was finally able to listen to the recording tonight. I was still processing what you told me. It was very powerful.

I've attached a picture of the clock that isn't working. My father mentioned it in my reading. The other pictures are of my parents when they were first married and when they celebrated their 50th wedding anniversary over 20 years ago. That was so funny that my father mentioned it. He always had a sense of humor.

Terry, you have given me a sense of peace and confirmed some things for me. You have a gift. Thank you for sharing it.

* * * * *

* * * * *

Hi Terry,

I wanted to send you a note on behalf of all of us.
Thank you from the bottom of our hearts for sharing
your talent with us.

It was a very special moment for us friends to connect
with our loved ones. You have given us great hope
and peace.

* * * * *

* * * * *

Theresa,

Thank you so much for meeting with me (us) today. I feel so blessed to have had a reading with you.

I had such an "Aha!" moment and am a bit mortified that I didn't put it together.

You had asked me if I knew a male Len/Lenny/Ken/Kenny. I brain-farted and said maybe it was my husband's friend but my maiden name is ████████ !! What a knucklehead I am!! That must have been my father trying to jump in.

Your gift is truly remarkable. If I can ever be of any assistance to you, please don't hesitate to reach out. I look forward to hearing the recording.

Thank you again. God bless you!

* * * * *

* * * * *

Hi Terry,

I hope you are well! I wanted to check in to see how you were doing and to let you know that ever since you came to bless my apartment all the weird stuff stopped!

I can not thank you enough!

I am interested in setting up a meeting with your friend Dawn. I want to try a psychic and see what those readings are like. Would you be able to share her contact info for me? I appreciate it!

Stay well.

* * * * *

* * * * *

Theresa,

Thank you so much for the awesome reading and also for taking extra time afterwards to talk with me.

I asked ███ today about the boys and she went over to the door, looked up pointing and said, "Look. See?" Like the kid was so relieved I acknowledged them. She kept saying, "Yellow. Yellow. Yellow". Then she went over looking for something and got a keychain and gave it to me. It's of a man (I think it's that iron superhero without the costume) and that just affirmed everything. Just amazing!

I can breathe so much better today and feel a weight has been lifted from my shoulders! I am so happy to know my grandma is enjoying food again after it being taken away for five years! It means the world to me! I can enjoy our holidays meals now and all her recipes so much more! Have a blessed day and wonderful holidays. I will definitely see you soon!

God bless you and thank you again so much! It was an honor meeting you!

* * * * *

Too Bad You're Going to Hell

A collection of stories and readings by

Spiritual Medium Theresa Marotta

Written by Heather T. Stone

This book is dedicated to my dad, Carmine Marotta.

If you didn't insist I place that ad during my visit to your gravesite I would never have used my gift to its fullest. It's because of you that I'm able to provide proof there is life, love and humor after the death transitioning.

Thank you for loving me… still.

This book is also dedicated to those of you who are brave enough to venture beyond your five primary senses to seek answers, love, comfort and knowledge that only the world beyond the veil can provide.

MEET THERESA

Thanksgiving 2011. My television debut. News Channel Four planned on airing the piece they did on my new cemetery business later in the day. The station thought it would be nice to have everyone remember their loved ones and think about them over the Thanksgiving table. I decided to host this year.

Family members began to arrive. Each one of them asked me if I was nervous. Believe it or not I wasn't. I was more concerned with figuring out how to fit everyone around the table so they'd all be comfortable. I was a little worried the camera would add ten pounds. Besides that I was fine. I believed in what I was doing and didn't care what the rest of the world thought. For the most part.

As in most Italian families, holiday meals are six to eight hour events. My children and grandchildren filled up my home with laughter and great conversation. The girls helped me bring food to the table and everyone took a seat. So far, so good. I turned the television to channel four and served the first course. Antipasto, pasta and pies were completely consumed. Not a single leftover. Now was the meal intermission. Turkey and all of the dressings would be next.

News Channel Four ran a brief commercial to show snippets of its upcoming program. When they mentioned the lady who visits cemeteries everyone in the room let out a cheer. I couldn't understand what all the fuss was about. I believed in what I was doing. Even if it was considered unusual.

My segment began with Maggie. The reporter had been a complete professional when he interviewed Maggie, an older woman who lived in New Jersey. Maggie was physically unable to visit her parents' and brother's grave sites since she was wheelchair bound. My cemetery business meant I would go in her place. The news clip, I believe, captured not only the essence of the respect behind the cemetery visits, but also showed the public that I wasn't there to mourn in their place. I was basically a delivery service who reported back the condition of the site.

When they filmed me they made me walk through the leaves on my way to Maggie's families grave site several times. Mind you, I'm pigeon toed and my boots were not made for walking. I was somewhat amused by the careful attention my walk garnered. It was, however, the only part that was staged. Other than that, I wasn't given any directions. No one told me what to say, how to say it or even when. Yet the words flowed through me like musical notes from a singer's mouth. I was guided by my dad and my spirit world.

After the clip was over, my family hugged and congratulated me. I was happy that I could be a source of pride for them that day. It was one more thing I was thankful for.

At the end of the piece one of the commentators remarked how nice it was of me to do this for others. I honestly never thought about it as being nice. I was grateful to have the opportunity to bridge the divide between those living and those who have passed.

While I was cleaning up the remnants of Thanksgiving dinner I couldn't help but think of my dad and what he said to me during his initial visit to me after his passing.

"Theresa, no one can take better care of you than me."

It was as true then as it is now. My father was the one that told me to start this business. He gave me the idea one day when I went to visit him in the cemetery. I didn't know at the time that one little message would change my life for the better.

My name is Theresa and I am an Intuitive Spiritual Medium. I've seen Spirit since childhood. You're about to hear my story from then until now.

When I was young any spirit that came to speak to me had to do all the work. They would have to show themselves physically, and speak to me using words - not images - as I was too young to understand that way. I didn't have the ability to speed up my vibrational energy. Now I can which makes it much easier for spirits to come through to me.

A medium is a person who can receive messages from Spirit. You first need to possess a psychic nature going beyond and using those senses we possess outside the five primary.

A medium needs to hone his or her psychic abilities to communicate and relay messages from Spirit. A medium needs to speed up his or her vibrational energy, the spirit needs to slow theirs down, and the meeting or exchange of information happens somewhere in the middle - or on the "medium" level.

A psychic differs from a medium. A psychic can go beyond some primary senses, but the messages are usually along the lines of telling whom ever they're reading their personality and past, present and future events. Not all psychics communicate with spirits. If they do, they're considered psychic mediums.

A medium usually doesn't "predict" future events. When doing readings, the client's loved ones come in just to prove they are still around and loving them. They can't interfere with free will. They can't interfere with any decisions we need to make. Free will reigns here and in their world.

I'm an Intuitive Medium because the spirits will use my physical body to tell their story. If, during a reading, I tell you I'm having a heart attack, I'm not. The spirit either had heart issues or died from a heart attack.

I'm a Spiritual Medium because the language they speak to me in is symbolism rooted in spirituality. Your loved ones will either show me a movie clip or images, put words in my mind, and sometimes they may even show me images of themselves. Communicating this way allows them to sustain energy throughout the reading.

When I do a reading, it's important that I'm able to let the client know what I see, hear or feel, and then I will look to them for clarity. If I say I had a heart attack, and that's what your loved one passed of, that's all the clarity I need. A simple, "Yes. That makes sense," will do. I don't give psychic readings so I'm not looking for information, only clarity. It's necessary since messages are often received backwards. Meaning most of the time we receive answers before we've figured out what the question was. They will give me the answer and I will need to seek the question (clarity).

When a client comes to me, I briefly explain that before any reading I go before my altar and say prayers. I know where the gift comes from, so I ask for God's guidance through his Arch Angels, Saints, and my loved ones who have passed before me. Now I'm not saying this is the right or wrong way to think, believe or pray. This is just *my* way. Your way may be different and that's okay. I say a prayer of protection, surround myself and my surroundings with white light and light candles. Any message that comes through must travel through all my layers of protection in order to reach me.

Sometimes the messages I relay can seem boring and mundane. However, the message itself proves they exist; they love us and they still look out for us.

I once read a woman of Chinese descent. She was amazed at the messages I gave her from her father. She said it had to be him because everything I'd told her was true, but she didn't understand how he could speak to me because he didn't speak English. That's when I learned messages from Spirit are already translated by the time they reach me.

Before the arrival of my client, I already have messages written for them through the prayer process. During a reading I have one steadfast rule; any spirit of a loved one that shows up must constantly throw out confirmations it's them. They may do so by telling me about a current event that happened after their passing, or an important memory in the person's life. I also let my client know their loved ones will speak using my language of symbolism which may differ from their own.

People who have passed communicate in different ways. Mediums receive messages different ways. There was a time I would watch mediums on television and be envious they could take part in question-and-answer sessions with spirits. My gift didn't work that way - at the time. But I practiced and fine tuned my gift and continue to learn new signs all the time.

Spirits need energy to sustain the lower vibrational level they need to be on for me to reach them. It's easier for them to put images in my mind as opposed to speaking into my ear as each action spends energy. Not that I don't hear the occasional sentence with my primary hearing, but mostly, I get images. Images and physical feelings. For example, I get a pain in the left side of my chest to mean heart attack. A pain in the right breast means breast cancer. The right side of my nose may run if someone is into drugs. You can find a more detailed list of my signs in Chapter Thirteen. Keep in mind these are *my* signs. Your signs would most likely be different.

When I do a reading, I have the person I'm reading choose a pencil from a box on the table. I have them rub it in their hands and hand it to me. I use it against yellow legal paper and usually begin with a few quick circles. The reading has begun!

I begin to tell the client signs and it's their job to give me clarity. I have no idea why I'm being shown statues of Buddha or a white toy rabbit on a shelf because it means nothing to me. But it may mean something to you. Most of the time I will never know if what I said was true. Clients don't normally pour their hearts out after a reading so there are a lot of times I leave the reading thinking I may not have done a good job - even though I've helped thousands of people.

Sometimes I receive a letter or email from an enlightened and satisfied client. They explain their life stories and how what I said to them gave them clarity, hope, or took weight off their shoulders. Some of their letters made their way into this book along with some of my favorite readings. Names have been changed or hidden to protect privacy.

The readings recorded in this book are as close to actual as possible while slightly cleaning up my Italian-from-the-Bronx accent and sentence structure. I was told it's impossible to have the latter and still be grammatically correct.

Enjoy!

Theresa Marotta

TABLE OF CONTENTS

Chapter 1

THE LADY IN WHITE

I grew up in the Bronx on Astor Avenue with my big, Roman Catholic, Italian family. My immediate family lived on the top floor of a two-family house owned by my grandmother. She lived downstairs with two of her daughters - my aunts. Grandma also owned the six family house on the same property. My uncle had one of those apartments.

With everyone so close, my childhood playmates included five siblings and seven first cousins. We lived together, stayed together, and all us kids played together every day. Between our two buildings was a big yard where we got to hang out when it was nice out. It was a great setup. Life was good.

Our house was old. It had a full-length attic that ran the entire length of our apartment below, accessible through a full set of stairs off the Television Room. We called it the Television Room because that was the only thing in the room. Well, technically there was a bookcase too, but no couch or chairs or anything else.

Once the house fell asleep, Dad and I would curl up on the floor with a blanket and watch that television. We'd watch our favorite anchorman read the day's news reports and when it was over, we'd both fall asleep to a late-night movie. This was our routine. Just me and Dad - as soon as Mom and my little sister went to sleep. Well, at least it was like that at first. As time passed on, I had to wait for Mom and all five siblings to pass out before I got my alone time with Dad.

When I was three years old, I used to go upstairs and into the attic to play or ride a little red tricycle my mom kept up there. The attic was the perfect place to ride it as it consisted of three rooms that connected to each other. One room was full of clothes being stored until the seasons changed - the type of clothes that cluttered up closets when the weather was warm. The middle room held lots of small knick-knacks and vintage kitchenware. Then there was a third and final room, but it wasn't on my route.

I loved that little red tricycle. I rode it all hours of the day; between the racks of sweaters and into the middle room, swing around the old typewriter, speed up near the pile of snow boots, hit a hard left and end up right where I started, which is precisely where I wanted to be so I could start again. It was so much fun. But, believe it or not, as fun as riding that little red tricycle was, it wasn't even the best part.

The most exciting part of my daily adventure was the anticipation of playing with my very own playmate, the Lady in White. I could always find her in the attic. She was a beautiful woman, about my mother's age. She had big brown eyes and the sweetest smile and always wore a long white dress. Not just any dress. It was always the same long, white dress. A gorgeous, long, white dress fit for a princess; the most remarkable dress my three-year-old eyes had ever seen. I loved the way it hung past her feet, making it seem as though she were floating. I never did learn her name, but it didn't matter. I referred to her as the Lady in White.

It's hard to explain how we met. She was always there since as far back as I was. My oldest memory of her was seeing her come out of the room that kept the out-of-season clothing. The room was full of those long types of stand-alone racks you see in retail shops today; each rack full. I'd go in there, start playing with my toys I kept there, and wait for her to appear.

The Lady in White was a kind woman who always had something nice to say. I couldn't tell you what her voice sounded like because we never used words to communicate. When we had something to tell each other we said it inside our heads - telepathically. She made me feel special; protected. I knew she loved me and I felt safe when she was around. She was a normal part of everyday life, for me, at least.

One day my little sister - the only sibling I had so far - wanted to come up in the attic with me. I didn't want to bring her to my special place, but she cried until my mother told me I had to bring her with me. I trudged upstairs with her in tow and started to explain the rules. As soon as we were high enough to see over the crest of the stairs, she took one look at the tricycle and ran full speed towards it. She tried to climb up too quickly and fell - flat on her face, bumping her chin on the handlebar on the way down. Luckily, the Lady in White was already here.

"Go get Mommy," my sister wailed.

"It's okay," I told her. "The Lady in White is here. She can help you."

She looked at me, took a long breath and let out another cry.

"Mommy!"

"Don't cry," I told her. "The Lady in White will help you."

I guess maybe she didn't like the Lady in White though I couldn't imagine why. The next thing I know she's climbing down the stairs, sobbing all the while. A few minutes later up comes Mom with that look on her face that said 'you're in big trouble little girl'.

"Theresa, why didn't you call me when your sister got hurt! You're the big sister. It's your job to watch over her."

"It's okay Mommy," I explained. "The Lady in White is here. She was watching over us."

"What do you mean the Lady in White is here?"

"She's right here." I pointed to her. She was standing in the corner next to a stack of boxes labeled "kitchen".

Mom looked confused. And still angry.

"The Lady in White is right here", I explained. "She was watching us, Mommy. I wasn't in charge."

My mother took a deep breath and walked downstairs without saying a word. A few minutes later she returned with a black-and-white photo I'd never seen before. She sat down in an old chair, held the photo out and asked a very simple question.

"Do you see the Lady in White?"

There were several people in the photo, but I noticed her right away and shook my head yes.

Mom took another deep breath. "Can you point to the Lady in White?"

I shook my head again and lifted my finger to the Lady in White.

"Are you sure?"

Of course I was. What kind of question was that? The Lady in White was now standing right next to me. Couldn't she see for herself?

That's when I realized she couldn't. Mom couldn't see the Lady in White. Neither could my little sister. No one could.

Mom looked tongue-tied. She just stood up, walked back downstairs and never talked about it again. It didn't bother me in the slightest. I still wanted to spend my special time with the Lady in White. I wasn't afraid of her even though no one could see her but me.

It's hard to explain what it's like to grow up with a third eye because it's normal to you. The Lady in White was a part of my day-to-day life, just like my other spiritual guide and protector, the Blessed Mother that lived in my backyard.

The tricycle wasn't the only reason I liked being in the attic. Out of the attic window, you could see the statue of the Madonna standing on a snake in a concrete block. My grandmother was devoted to Our Lady and put that statue there the day she moved in. However, at the age of three, I had no concept of what religion was. I didn't know my grandmother was devoted to the Blessed Mother, or that the statue was so old, put into place so long ago that the sun washed away all traces of its original coloring, leaving it a creamy white. It was because of Her coloring that I also referred to Her as the Lady in White. She was also my friend whom I talked to often.

I worried about Her sometimes, always standing on a snake. I asked Her if it hurt. She said it didn't. I asked Her why She stood on it and why it didn't hurt and why She always had "sparkles" fluttering around Her head.

"In time you'll know. In time you'll understand," was Her answer. "The timing isn't right for you now. Wait until you're older."

She was right. Back then I was too young to understand what was happening - why I could see and hear things other people couldn't. I was too young to understand why my mother never mentioned that day in the attic or the Lady in White ever again, but her actions were enough to warrant me never to bring it up either. I kept my secret gift to myself and continued to grow up intuitive, believing there was something wrong with me.

Chapter 1 ½

BECKY'S READING

Theresa: Alright, so have a seat. We're good to go. In that box are the pencils. Choose one, please. Rub it between both hands and hand it to me. Now, before you got here I went before my altar and this is what I get. You live in Carmel so maybe this is it. Do you go up the Taconic Parkway or Route 22?

Becky: The Taconic.

Theresa: Okay. There was a spirit that was in the car with you and I only see the treetops, not the road, like I'm not tall enough to see out the window. It's a recent trip. I'm in the back seat behind the passenger. I'm going to see who this spirit is. I do know it's male, not female. But there is a female coming through also now. Who had breast cancer?

Becky: My Aunt ███████████.

Theresa: She's one of the spirits in the car. She wants to be acknowledged first. She's running in to be acknowledged. You also have a grandfather there as well. He was also in the car. Is your grandfather on the other side?

Becky: One of them, yeah. I have three. My parents are divorced.

Theresa: Well, your grandfather was running in also. Everyone is running in, for some reason, for you. They're all *running* in. So I don't know whether you almost had a change of heart coming here or…

Becky: Yes! That's so funny. I got busy, and I thought maybe I should reschedule.

Theresa: Oh okay. So they weren't 100% sure you would keep this appointment. Now they're rushing to get here. They're showing me a home they visit. This home has two windows but there's a wall separating them. I see one window, the wall, then another window. I feel like I'm you or your mom that I'm coming to visit. Who has the two windows in their room? But the windows aren't side by side so it doesn't make a double window.

Becky: In my room, the two walls that connect each have a window.

Theresa: Okay. But the windows don't form a double window?

Becky: Right.

Theresa: Cool. So far I know that this aunt or grandfather is showing me your room. Because I know I'm either attached to you or your mother. They want me to mention the month of May. So let's go with the month of May. Either the month itself means something, the fifth of any month or the name Mary or Maria; first, middle, last name or nickname.

Becky: My grandmother is Maria.

Theresa: Is Grandma still with us?

Becky: No.

Theresa: She's on the other side. Okay, cool.

Becky: She'd definitely be knocking people over to get through.

Theresa: There's someone else who's here, she's saying. So let's go back to the Month of May. It's either May, the fifth of any month, the name Mary or Maria. Now Mary or Maria can be part of a name - like Anne Marie or Maria-Rose. Your grandmother is saying 'there's another one'.

Becky: My grandmother's name is Maria, but I can't think of May.

Theresa: There's another lady with your grandmother.

Becky: Her sister.

Theresa: Oh okay. There ya go. I'm equal to her. And now I'm getting cramps in my foot. One of these two ladies used to suffer with either the leg or the foot, but they're also pointing to this side (meaning alive). Now, Mom is still with us, right?

Becky: Yeah.

Theresa: Is she getting cramps in her feet?

Becky: They swell. A lot.

Theresa: She needs to drink. . . tonic wa. . .? No. *Theresa pauses and tries to make sense of the sign she's being shown.* It's either tonic water or club soda.

Becky: She does drink club soda for it. I just got so dizzy.

Theresa: They're here. So you're reacting to them. Perfect. When these ladies come they're stronger than your grandfather.

Becky: Yeah, I was a lot closer to them.

Theresa: You know when you're driving up a mountain and your ears pop?

Becky: Yeah.

Theresa: When the spirits start coming through, we get dizzy. It changes the atmosphere. You are so protected here you have nothing to worry about. Nothing. Okay? Plus, it's love that's coming through. Something with Crestwood. Do you even know where Crestwood is?

Becky: No.

Theresa: That could be Crestwood Avenue? Or we have a section down in Yonkers. Did anybody come from Yonkers?

Becky: Yes. My mom and her whole side of the family are from Yonkers.

Theresa: Do you know where?

Becky: Kimball Ave. But they're all alive

Theresa: Yeah I know, that's fine. But this is Crestwood. That's off Central Avenue. There's a connection there.

Becky: I do know where that is, actually. But I can't think of the connection.

Theresa: Don't worry about it. That's why I give you this paper. I have to mention the month of April.

Becky: That's my birthday.

Theresa: Yes. The month of April was all over you, the minute you walked in. Actually, when I came in here to prepare the room, I heard this lady saying "April, April, April," and I'm thinking (don't even ask me why. I should know.) why April? Out of all the months; not even putting one and one together that it could be related to you. Who's Annabelle?

Becky: Annabelle! Oh my gosh! I was with my boyfriend earlier. That's why I didn't know if I was going to be on time. He was saying he was hoping I would meet his grandmother. She's passed.

Theresa: She's here.

Becky: Her name was Annabelle.

Theresa: See? She came before you even got here. I didn't even start reading your pencil yet, and she came in during the prayer part. Who had the heart problems or carotid vein problems? My carotid artery is bothering me, so this could be high cholesterol or heart problems - not a heart attack.

Becky: My step dad's father.

Theresa: He is on the other side.

Becky: Yes.

Theresa: Okay he's here also. Have you been praying a lot? Or thinking more about a higher being or angels?

Becky: Yes.

Theresa: Okay. Because when you even open yourself up a little, even to the thought of them, you open a window for love to come through. You're not opening a window just for any soul or any spirit, so don't worry about who can show up. It's only love that's here for you.

Becky: Wow, that's so funny. I wanted to get back into going to church.

Theresa: You should.

Becky: And I talk to my relatives on the other side, out loud, when I'm alone. I always feel like I'm not alone in my house because being alone in my house freaks me out.

Theresa: No. They're always around you.

Becky: I feel like I see things and when I look there's nothing to see.

Theresa: There is nothing negative around you. As a matter of fact, Archangel Michael, whom I always call to me, is here. He knows what's going on. He's sending healing energy through Archangel Raphael to someone in the family. Someone needs healing. I don't think it's medical. I think it's more emotional or mental. But I'm not you. It's not you he's sending it to. It is someone whose energy bounces off you. So, I'm around you. I don't know if I'm your mom or...

Becky: It could be a couple. They all need it.

Theresa: Your grandfather's showing me garbage trucks, or the carting service. Was anyone a garbage man? They're showing me these big trucks.

Becky: No. But I was thinking about calling. I work in sales and it's for energy and I was thinking of calling a carting company, but I didn't know if it was a good idea.

Theresa: It is a good idea. So they already answered that for you. Wow.

Becky: Okay.

Theresa: He has what he's calling the big dog. It could be a dog like a boxer size.

Becky: I have a big dog. And he's named after that grandfather. We named him Charlie.

Theresa: Come on, seriously? There ya go. Who's thinking about the new car?

Becky: Me.

Theresa: What kind of car are you thinking about getting?

Becky: A Subaru.

Theresa: Okay, they said 'yes'. Very good. Why are your loved ones talking about the pig roast?

Becky: I haven't done a pig roast since college.

Theresa: Okay, hold on. So they're showing me a memory. Remember that they come through with confirmations regarding either a current event or a memory. Was your grandfather on the other side when you had them?

Becky: Yes.

Theresa: Okay. Well, guess what? Grandpa was hanging out there. Oh! The number eight, big time. This is either August, the eighth of any month, or the number eight.

Becky: I can't think of anything.

Theresa: He's sticking with it so I have to figure it out. Was there an event that happened in August after he passed? We were just talking about the pig roast so I think he wants to tell you he was there. August, the eighth of any month, or the number eight.

Becky: Years ago, my mother went to a medium. My sister, well my step-sister, has issues with drugs and they told her that she needed to be careful because something bad was going to happen in August or the eighth. It was always eight.

Theresa: And nothing happened.

Becky: So far nothing's happened.

Theresa: It's not going to happen. That's bullshit.

Becky: Oh that's good.

Theresa: Because can I tell you something? If you're working from the light you're not giving messages like that. You can say things like, 'listen, there's someone around you that's using drugs. They have to be a little careful.' Because they usually don't show the end result. And I don't want to know; that's my deal. But this August or the eighth is in the middle of everyone's business. Did anyone have six kids because that would make it a family of eight?

Becky: No.

Theresa: Okay. I'm going to stick with it. You see how clear you see the eight? *Theresa points to where her pencil lines made a number eight in the middle of several random circles*

Becky: Mmhmm.

Theresa: It's in the middle of people's business. Keep that in mind. You have to give me another pencil and rub it. He's showing me - whose nickname was either

Spitfire or Firecracker; if I was describing a personality?

Becky: Grandma. Or it could've been his sister, my aunt.

Theresa: Do you know Big Al or Al?

Becky: Yeah. That's my mom's father. Grandpa. But he's here.

Theresa: Okay. So they're saying hello to him. I hear the name. I didn't see or feel anyone new so I don't know where he is. They're saying hello to him. Did he have an injury on his foot?

Becky: Yes.

Theresa: They have to give me confirmation that's who they're referring to. Who makes the dish with the potatoes? I don't know.

Becky: I don't know. It could be any one of us.

Theresa: Oh potatoes are big for you?

Becky: Yeah.

Theresa: Okay. It's not french fries. It's some kind of specialized side dish with potatoes?

Becky: Hmm.

Theresa: Don't go too far. I'm either you or your mother. I'm close to you.

Becky: I just made, for the first time, roasted potatoes.

Theresa: There ya go. For the first time. Did they come out good?

Becky: No.

Theresa: Because you forgot some stuff. Did you put the rosemary on it?

Becky: No.

Theresa: That's one of the things your grandmother said you forgot. Who's Robert or Bob?

Becky: My boyfriend's father's name is Robert. We call him Bob.

Theresa: There's a woman on the other side for him.

Becky: That would be Annabelle.

Theresa: She's still watching over him. He doesn't realize it but he still calls out to her. How long ago did she pass?

Becky: A while.

Theresa: Oh okay. That's why he doesn't know that he's still calling out to her. Who has - we used to call it a bay window, but it's a protruding window?

Becky: He does.

Theresa: How good are these people at giving me these confirmations? They're bringing in Saint Teresa, big time, for you. Now let me tell you, when I see Saint Teresa, what it means to me. Either the month of October means something to someone. October or the tenth of any month or someone used to live near a church.

Becky: My grandmother Maria passed in October and lived across from a church.

Theresa: She travels with Saint Teresa. Not Mother Teresa. She's being very clear about this and she wants you to know you have Saint Teresa's eyes. And she's right. You do. I have a picture of the real Saint Teresa and you have the eyes. Is someone in construction cause I'm hearing GC? Now that could be a general contractor, the initials GC or CG.

Becky: I can't think of anything.

Theresa: Okay. I'm going back to the GC because that was the first one I went to. Is anyone thinking about doing renovations to their house?

Becky: My brother. He just bought a house.

Theresa: Okay. That makes sense. Did he do his homework on the GC? They want to know. Who's running the construction?

Becky: He is.

Theresa: Okay. So he better do his homework. They're right. Who's ███ ?

Becky: That's my cousin.

Theresa: What's his story? They're mentioning ██████.
What's going on near ██████?

Becky: We're not very close. He doesn't live close and
he doesn't keep in touch.

Theresa: I think you're going to hear something.

Becky: Oh he does! He flips houses.

Theresa: Get the frig out of here!

Becky: He flips homes. Him and his wife.

Theresa: You're going to hear something from him or
about him.

Becky: Oh. I wonder if he's going to have a baby
because they've been trying.

Theresa: I don't know. They should pray to Saint Ann.
Saint Ann is the patron Saint for that. If you have a
problem conceiving or having a baby, you pray to
Saint Ann. *Takes a deep breath.* ██████.

Becky: My cousin.

Theresa: They're asking about him.

Becky: The women?

Theresa: Yeah. Why?

Becky: I'm not very close with him. I don't have
communication really with my father. And that would
be his brother's son.

Theresa: Something's coming up. It's almost like things are ready to erupt or come together. Now, eruptions don't necessarily mean a bad thing; it brings new life to something. It expands. Not in a bad way, because they're coming with good messages. They're not coming with bad messages. Oh, I'm nauseous. Who had the cancer?

Becky: Aunt Estelle had cancer.

Theresa: Oh okay. She wants to talk again. Who's █████?

Becky: █████ is another cousin.

Theresa: She's talking about █████ for some reason. I know it's odd. But she's mentioning her. Now it's almost like I'm in some kind of trouble. Not with the cops or medically. It's like something is upsetting me. Now, are you close to █████ or no?

Becky: Not really, but I see her.

Theresa: There's a problem near █████. Now, your aunt is saying, 'It's not your problem, but you're going to hear about it'. Who puts the broom in the closet?

Becky: I don't know.

Theresa: Not a clothes closet, but this aunt is showing me I put this broom in the closet. Could be a kitchen thing. I put the broom in the closet.

Becky: My grandmother did. She had a tall thing in her kitchen.

Theresa: Do you have the vacuum? Because there's going to be a problem with a vacuum. She's just giving you a heads up. Do you burn your candles?

Becky: I haven't in a while.

Theresa: Please start again because they loved that. Use scented candles. They don't want you to overdo it. So who was thinking about painting?

Becky: My brother. In the new place.

Theresa: Oh okay. So they're just giving me clarity. There's a baby boy here. But this boy was never alive. No one miscarried. I'm ready to come, somehow, into this family. There's going to be an engagement or wedding coming up. They already know about it but they're not showing me who. The number sixteen. So this could be near the sixteenth of a month or I could be the age sixteen.

Becky: My sister's birthday is the sixteenth. The one with the drug problem.

Theresa: Does she listen to music?

Becky: Yeah.

Theresa: Does she listen to music with headphones?

Becky: I don't know.

Theresa: They want you to know that when she listens to music, it's a form of therapy. So the music will help her with something. Get it out of your mind that she's going to pass from drugs. Whatever that medium told you would have already happened, if in fact. Okay? And it's irresponsible for her to instill fear. A medium's job is not to create fear or dependency like, 'there is a curse on you'. That's such bullshit. So just get rid of that thought. I'm now seeing either bubbles or balloons.

Becky: I just got balloons for my dad. It's his birthday.

Theresa: Oh okay. Someone's being a baboon. It's not your father. But I'm being an ass. I'm being primal. I'm a male. I think I'm being very protective of the female, but I might as well lift up my leg and pee on her. I'm being territorial. There's a baboon energy in the family. There's this male. They don't like this energy. You'll know who it is. Don't think too hard about it. You'll know. This is going to be someone relatively new. Someone that either just came near the family or is going to come near the family. Who used to wear the costume jewelry?

Becky: My grandmother did.

Theresa: She did. Oh the pennies. You know, it's so funny because I don't like cliches - that "pennies from heaven thing" - because I'm too Bronxy for that, but your grandmother is claiming pennies. Have you been finding them?

Becky: There's this one on the counter this morning. It's been there all day and all I kept thinking was what the hell is this doing there?

Theresa: You know what. Hold on to it and put it in a special box. It's from her. Wow. See what I make fun of they make me swallow. It's too cliche for me. I don't like it. But she's saying keep the penny. There's a creative energy near you. I'm hoping you're going to do something with it. May I ask what you do for a living?

Becky: I sell energy. I work for an energy supply company. It's not what I want to do.

Theresa: There's going to be a Bronx connection surrounding you. Where's your boyfriend's father from?

Becky: From Yonkers, but right on the border of the Bronx.

Theresa: Okay. It's a good thing. I'm hoping you're happy because they are too. They are mentioning Fridays. So either someone does something on Fridays or used to do something on Fridays.

Becky: My nephew comes over on Fridays. From my sister. The one with the addiction. Her son.

Theresa: How old is he?

Becky: Ah ha! He's going to be eight.

Theresa: There ya go. This poor kid is in the middle of a lot of stuff. Remember when I said the number eight is in the middle of everyone's business? They want you to know that they're watching over him.

Becky: He's probably the one that needs the healing.

Theresa: There ya go. Okay. Oh, I just got the chills. Do you get bronchitis or cough or sore throats?

Becky: I do. I always get bronchitis.

Theresa: Because your grandmother… do you have two? Well, the grandmother and the sister because they're coming in alike.

Becky: She was like my grandmother because my grandmother passed when I was young.

Theresa: That's why they're both coming in. They lay their hands on your throat. It's indicative of what area in the body has energy that's weak. Once you start wearing a scarf, you can't stop until it's warm out. That's what they're saying. The color black for you is a power color. It doesn't drain your energy. They are bringing the green near you though. Green is a healing color. Not that you need healing, but whose patron Saint was Saint Jude or who gives to Saint Jude?

Becky: My mom gives to Saint Jude because I volunteered for them for a long time.

Theresa: Did you?

Becky: Yeah, in college.

Theresa: Oh okay because his color, Saint Jude, is green. And obviously, he's healing. They're just giving me a memory. Now they're showing me little sticky things that can stick to your clothes. They look like little burrs. I don't know what it is. Now there's either a story attached to it or this poor thing is always getting stuck in it.

Becky: I can't remember exactly who, but we would go to their house, a relative and they would have bushes like that. I think it was in Yonkers. But they're all alive.

Theresa: Yeah it's okay. Maybe they want you to know they visit there.

Becky: Yeah. We always had to pick them off.

Theresa: Is there a woman living there?

Becky: Yes.

Theresa: How old is that woman?

Becky: Now, in her seventies.

Theresa: They need her eyes to get checked. That's all they're saying. It's not a bad thing. Her eyes need to be checked. I'm still chuckling about the number eight.

Becky: Yeah. It didn't hit me until you mentioned it.

Theresa: It wasn't meant to hit you then. That's how this works. They just keep leading until the full revelation is acknowledged. I have to trust them and then it's even a revelation to me. Who's my PB&J person? I love peanut butter and jelly.

Becky: Maybe my brother?

Theresa: No. I don't pick that up. I'm either going to your boyfriend or your boyfriend's father because it's Annabelle saying it.

Becky: I don't know. I don't think I even know them well enough yet.

Theresa: You may find out. Who's Betty or Elizabeth; because Betty is short for Elizabeth?

Becky: Betty is my great uncle's wife who passed when I was young.

Theresa: She's here also. Not seashells, but do you collect rocks? Like, from the water? Or the ocean?

Becky: I have.

Theresa: What do you do with them?

Becky: I have them out on my dresser.

Theresa: Good. The rocks have life in them because they came from the water. The currency of the water keeps the spirits coming and going. They're putting Saint John near you.

Becky: John's my boyfriend.

Theresa: There you go. But does someone have something with Buddha?

Becky: Me.

Theresa: Can you explain that?

Becky: I have them all over my room.

Theresa: This is what they see when they come. Your energy goes more toward collecting them and not into the religion they represent.

Becky: Yes.

Theresa: But just so you know, even if you believed in them that's fine. It's all the same. As long as you believe in a higher being. Do you have a picture of you and your grandmother when you were young?

Becky: Yeah.

Theresa: Do you know where that picture is?

Becky: It's hanging in my room.

Theresa: Oh that's where it is? Good. It should stay out. Okay. Now they're showing me someone wearing something that they think are pants (this is a female) and they're not. So it could be those leggings or it can be the pajama things and you wear them out.

Becky: That's me!

Theresa: Drives your grandmother nuts.

Becky: I'm sure it does.

Theresa: Then the other thing... it's a 'J' but it's a weird 'J' name. It's either Jeremy.

Becky: My brother.

Theresa: They send love to him. Do you know a Jack yet?

Becky: Jack lives next door. My neighbor's son.

Theresa: They're watching over him. They talk about a bakery shop. Now, either someone used to go to a bakery shop, or was a baker.

Becky: My uncle, Betty's husband was a baker.

Theresa: Okay. And he's on the other side.

Becky: No.

Theresa: Oh. He's here?

Becky: Oh wait! He is on the other side. Oh, my goodness! Uncle Bob.

Theresa: Oh okay. Because I was going to say maybe they have a son the same name. You're not thinking of becoming a jogger, are you?

Becky: Yes I am.

Theresa: They're saying make sure you limber up enough. You did great. They're very strong.

Chapter 2

MEET BENITA

I met Benita, Nita for short, in my mid-fifties. By then I was the mother of three grown children, grandmother to four beautiful grandchildren and an ex-wife to three men.

My oldest child made the medical books because he was born without a thyroid gland. Not a low functioning thyroid. He was born with no gland at all. It's because of his condition that they test all babies born in the United States for thyroid function. He had some developmental issues when he was young so I was needed home to help him through his everyday life. While I was a stay-at-home mom, I gathered up various licenses so I'd be ready to re-enter the workforce when the time came when my children no longer needed me twenty-four hours a day.

I became a Notary, Paralegal, Real Estate Salesperson, Bookkeeper; I even held a Private Detective's license. Every single one of these licenses helped me seek and find work. They also afforded me the luxury of helping my son financially so he could become comfortable in his newfound life outside my home.

My last job before being "pushed" to use my gift full time was as a bookkeeper for a retail store. About a year after I started, the company lost their Buying Agent and they hired Nita shortly after. I met her briefly as she adjusted to her office directly next to mine. After that day I barely ever saw her. She was busy with her new workload and I had a ton of my own things to take care of. So when the office wanted to go in on group lottery tickets for the big jackpot I used it as an excuse to strike up a conversation.

I popped my head in, smiled and said hello.

"Jackpot drawing is tonight. It's up to seventy-mill. The office is getting tickets. Would you like to get in?"

She met my gaze and returned with a polite grin. "No, thank you."

"You sure? It's only a few dollars. You wouldn't want to be the only one to come to work if we win, right?"

"No, thank you," she reiterated. "It's against my religion."

"Oh, yeah?" I stepped a little further into her office and leaned back against the doorway. "Do you mind if I ask what your faith is?"

"I'm Pentecostal. I don't believe in gambling."

"Wow, you're only the second Pentecostal I've ever met in my entire life. My husband is Pentecostal as well."

There was no way this was a coincidence. My life experiences have taught me not to believe in coincidences as the spiritual realm designed them for our benefit. Meaning there's a meaning. I didn't know how this meeting would play into that belief, but I remained open to the thought.

Pentecostalism is a movement within Protestant Christianity that emphasizes direct contact with God through Baptism of the Holy Spirit. While the beliefs vary by denomination, several similarities include: Rejection of the Trinity, believing in one energy as opposed to three separate beings (I.e., the Father, the Son and the Holy Spirit); practicing modesty adhering to strict guidelines like women can't wear skirts shorter than the bottom of their knees and men can't have hair that reaches their shoulders. They also believe in Baptism by the Holy Spirit. Those who are "saved" may also speak in tongue. Some people believe the Gift of Tongue is a direct connection to God and the speaker is channeling true words from the divine - although his words could be completely incomprehensible. Others believe speaking in tongue is a private way to pray to the "man upstairs" as only He will be able to decipher the true meaning of the spoken gibberish.

"That's very interesting. I was raised Roman Catholic." We chatted a few more minutes and I was out the door and down the hall to finish a day's work and go home.

We continued to chat each morning. I'd pop into her office and catch up on the previous day's work. We'd shoot the breeze a bit then carry out our days in our offices. A good friendship was forming as we became part of each other's daily routines. Nita was a sweetheart that put the world before herself and I enjoyed her company.

Then the day came when she was comfortable enough with me to really let me know how she felt. It was 9:20 on a Monday morning. I was sitting in a chair in front of her desk - half a cup of coffee left, still half asleep. We were talking about something that happened to Nita in Church. She looks me in the eye, lowered her voice and whispered. "Word around the work grapevine is you're a psychic."

"I'm not a psychic. I'm a medium."

"What does that mean?"

"It means I can communicate with energies that have passed."

Nita's face turned red. She looked horrified. She also looked like she was struggling to breathe - though I knew she could since she was able to blurt out the word "Brujah" which is Spanish for witch.

"I do NOT believe in these kinds of things. Look, Terry, you're a nice person, but I can't believe you do the devil's work. Keep that away from me. I'll pray for you."

Now, most people might be a little taken back by a comment like that. Think about how you'd feel if your new co-worker just verbally accused you of worshiping the devil. Then add in my Italian from the Bronx attitude and you're in for a blowout. I could have told her the truth. I could've told her I've seen the other side and Heaven. Who was she to tell me anything? I knew the truth. The Blessed Mother talks to me personally. Pray for me? You should be asking me to pray for you.

But I refrained, bit my tongue, and accepted that she was only condemning me due to her own fear and misunderstanding. It's difficult to accept what you don't understand, especially when it's something that goes against your faith. I could understand where she came from. After all, I was raised by devout Catholics who believe that if you follow the rules - and only if you followed the rules - you make it to heaven. Unfortunately for them, I've been a rule breaker since childhood.

Chapter 2 ½

LAURIE'S READING

Theresa: Before we get started I just want to acknowledge that your grandmother came through with lung issues. Hand me the pencil. This isn't going to be a religious reading. It will be spiritual though, okay?

Laurie: Okay.

Theresa: They gave me the month of December. Let me tell you about my months. It's either December, the month itself means something, the twelfth of any month, or the number twelve. Why did they give me December?

Laurie: December twelfth is my birthday.

Theresa: Your grandmother comes through big time. She is your guardian. Now, your grandmother is telling me she isn't a guardian angel because, believe it or not, angels were created for our benefit. She doesn't want to get demoted. She's got a little bit of an ego going on.

Laurie: Yeah she does.

Theresa: It's also not a coincidence that she spoke to you today with the colors that you're wearing. First, there are no coincidences. You have the color of December on you. It's also the color of Archangel Michael.

Laurie: Oh wow. I didn't even know that.

Theresa: What else, other than the color of December? Why would your grandma tell me it's not a coincidence that you chose these colors?

Laurie: I don't know.

Theresa: Well, I know this is representative of December. They speak to us using our gut feelings. You might think to yourself, "Oh, I just feel like putting this on. It feels right." Whenever something feels right, that's your grandmother. If you're having a hard time making a decision, that's on you. So listen to your gut feeling because now it's your grandmother. She has a dog with her. She's just bringing in this dog. It's a mid-sized dog. Back in the day who had this dog? I think it was a mutt because it doesn't look like a purebred.

Laurie: Her son.

Theresa: Okay. But the dog has passed.

Laurie: Yeah. I have the dog's sister.

Theresa: Oh do you? Good. When Grandma comes to visit, she brings the dog with her. What you're going to start noticing is with the dog you have, is that your dog will suddenly become alert. It could be sleeping and just raise its head and stare at nothing.

And you're saying, what the frig is this dog looking at? It's the other dog.

Laurie: Oh wow.

Theresa: The month of September. So either the month of September means something, the ninth of any month, the number nine or the name Michael first, middle, last or nickname.

Laurie: Well there was ███████████ Michael. That's my aunt. That's her daughter.

Theresa: Okay. And the daughter's still here?

Laurie: Yeah.

Theresa: She wants you to reach out to that daughter, but she's making me feel like the energy in her back is off.

Laurie: Oh wow.

Theresa: Alright, so it might be a little achy or something. It's something that she's doing. It's not a medical reason. It's either I'm stretching the wrong way or I'm lifting wrong. She's telling you to make sure you tell her. Now she's showing me bird eggs. I've never seen this so... who either was *Theresa starts to cough.* Is your grandfather on the other side?

Laurie: Yes.

Theresa: Okay. Because she's telling me to tell you your grandfather's here. He's here for a reason. Your grandmother's speaking to me. He's just standing there behind her. Okay. The bird eggs. Who either used to feed birds? *Theresa's right nostril starts to run.* Oh, this my sign for drugs. Can you please pass me a tissue? Who used to do the drugs or does drugs? It's either pot or cocaine.

Laurie: My sister does pot.

Theresa: My nose won't run again since we were able to acknowledge the sign. Grandma is not judging her, but she's disappointed.

Laurie: Yeah

Theresa: Again, she's not judging. She loves her. But she's disappointed because your sister has so much she can give. And if she thinks it's not doing her any harm, she's crazy. That's what your grandmother's saying. Why does she put a police officer near you? Who in the family is a cop or I go to work in a uniform?

Laurie: My dad's a security officer.

Theresa: There you go. She's saying hello to him. Now, dad's still with us?

Laurie: Yes.

Theresa: Okay. She does care for your father, but there was some kind of problem there.

Laurie: Oh yeah.

Theresa: They don't take the problems with them to the other side. She's going to try to help him out with something though. Watermelon. Who's my watermelon person?

Laurie: My uncle in Detroit. Her daughter's husband.

Theresa: Her daughter's husband. He's still with us?

Laurie: Yeah.

Theresa: She goes there to visit as well. Someone was recently watching a tv show or a movie. I'm home. I'm not in a movie theater. And I was thinking of someone who passed. So the movie or the tv show either reminded me of this person or I was sitting there and I'm trying to watch it, but I'm thinking. And your grandmother makes me feel it was about her.

Laurie: I always do. I'm a movie person so it had to be me.

Theresa: Okay. Let me go onto this. There is a father type energy. This is your father type energy. Your father type energy would be your grandfather because he's coming in through your dad. Was he distant? Or was he not around a lot?

Laurie: Yeah. I didn't know him.

Theresa: Okay. So he's introducing himself to you. He's talking about the pickle person.

Laurie: Oh my God! I have no idea who the pickle person is, but I knew he liked pickles.

Theresa: Oh. So he was the pickle person! That's why he's talking about it. Who used to have hip problems? A woman with hip problems.

Laurie: A woman with hip problems? The only person I know would be my grandmother.

Theresa: Oh okay. It would be her.

Laurie: Yeah. She had a lot of problems.

Theresa: Okay. Remember that they have to constantly throw out confirmations that it's them. Now some people ask me why do you give such mundane messages? Because it proves that it's your loved ones and that they know what is currently happening in your life. You're supposed to be in a criminal field or a cop or in uniform. What do you do right now?

Laurie: I want to be a paramedic.

Theresa: Oh alright. So you will be in a uniform. That's fine. So we talked about the drugs. We did the dog. Whose initial is "D", first, middle, last or nickname? This person is alive. I'm not passed.

Laurie: D? There's D█████████

Theresa: Who's D█████████? We always go with our first instinct.

Laurie: Her cousin.

Theresa: Now what's going on with D█████████? There's a problem?

Laurie: I wouldn't be able to tell you.

Theresa: Now is D█████████████ related to this grandmother?

Laurie: Yeah.

Theresa: Okay. Then it is her. There's a problem. It's not an emergency problem. She has to find her way out of a paper bag right now. So she's dealing with something. I have an uncle coming in now.

Laurie: Yes.

Theresa: Okay. Do you have an uncle on the other side that's related to your father?

Laurie: No. Not that I would know of.

Theresa: Because he's standing near your father's father.

Laurie: I mean, they lived near each other. My grandmother's son just passed a couple years back.

Theresa: From what?

Laurie: From an infection. He had a lung virus.

Theresa: No. It's not him. So that's like an uncle or if he had a cousin or somebody that would have been older.

Laurie: Older, older? He did have a cousin that was married to my mom's sister that passed from kidney failure.

Theresa: Oh. So your father's cousin married your mother's sister. Okay. That's why I'm a little confused.

Laurie: Yeah. It's a big family.

Theresa: I do know that he's standing next to your grandfather who is your father's father. At one point, he was either in an accident or hurt his chest on something. He's talking about a key. Did you lose a key? Are you having a problem with a certain key? There's something with a key or a key needs to be replaced.

Laurie: I lost the link to a key.

Theresa: When?

Laurie: A couple weeks ago.

Theresa: What was going on because that's when this gentleman started coming. He's giving me headaches. He helped your grandfather get to you. Now, who's there longer, the cousin or the grandfather?

Laurie: The grandfather.

Theresa: Why is he helping your grandfather get to you? Did you know the cousin more than you knew the grandfather?

Laurie: He was like my neighbor.

Theresa: Oh, that's why. So that's why he helps the grandfather. I'm near the twenty third of a month. So that could mean twenty-second, twenty-third, twenty-fourth.

Laurie: Yes.

Theresa: Why?

Laurie: May twenty-third. It's like, the most dominant birthday we have.

Theresa: Oh okay. It's their sign that they're definitely with you. Your grandmother wants to speak again.

Laurie: What?

Theresa: I'm sorry. She's talking about wonton soup. Who eats the Chinese food all the time?

Laurie: Her daughter.

Theresa: She's trying new things, your grandmother's saying. Your grandmother knows that she's trying new things. Boy she flies all over the place. She gave me a really big confirmation with the twenty-third. She just interrupted those gentlemen I was speaking to and started talking. Now I have anxiety. Who suffers from anxiety?

Laurie: The one who does drugs.

Theresa: Your sister. Oh, this poor thing. She's really hurting herself. She doesn't even see what she's doing to the family.

Laurie: No. She doesn't. Never.

Theresa: Grandma's showing me a cab. Was someone recently in a cab?

Laurie: She was. My dad took the car away from her.

Theresa: So she has to use a cab now. Grandma knows this and is showing this as a current event. Oh and the smell! When your grandmother comes, this is going to be cool, it's the smell of apples.

Laurie: That's funny because we're going apple picking.

Theresa: No way!

Laurie: And I don't even like apples.

Theresa: No way. You're going apple picking?

Laurie: Yeah. The seventh. It's a whole family thing.

Theresa: Grandma will be there. That's why it's going to be the smell of apples for her. Obviously not when you have apples in the house, she's saying. You cry in the shower?

Laurie: Sometimes.

Theresa: She shows me this. Crying is healing, she's saying. You're supposed to get a new car or someone's getting a car.

Laurie: I just got a new car.

Theresa: When?

Laurie: April.

Theresa: She was there when you chose it. You're going to find loose coins in it. In the car. I think she's going to give like a penny, a nickel, a dime, a quarter.

Laurie: Ah huh.

Theresa: Whenever you find the loose change - not when you drop change because then we know where it comes from - just random change. Please save those coins. She does sit next to you in the car. So if you want to have a conversation with her telepathically, you can. Either someone is suffering with sinuses or is constantly sniffling.

Laurie: My sister. My other one.

Theresa: So that's how she reaches out to that sister. Who's Jean Jane, Gina? Who's this? I'm alive. Do you have a friend named Jane, Jean, Gina, first, middle, last name or nickname? It could be Jeanmarie. It sounds like "G" "J" sound.

Laurie: "J"? There's Joseph.

Theresa: No. This is female.

Laurie: I don't know anybody with a "J". Or a Jean sound that comes to mind.

Theresa: Alright. Who at work has that name?

Laurie: Jean-███████.

Theresa: Who's this?

Laurie: She's my boss. I take care of her twin boys.

Theresa: Grandma is going back to May. Who's associated with May?

Laurie: Well, most of my family.

Theresa: No, it's the name Maria. Who's Maria?

Laurie: Maria?

Theresa: It could be Annmarie. Maria something.

Laurie: Is she a neighbor?

Theresa: It could be.

Laurie: A neighbor.

Theresa: Did grandma know her?

Laurie: Yeah.

Theresa: Okay, I can go there then. Grandma visits that house.

Laurie: Oh wow. That's her old house!

Theresa: She watches over there. She makes sure everything is okay. She's showing me dirty water. There's going to be a leak, something with the pipes.

Laurie: Oh wow. There was water leaking there.

Theresa: Oh okay. Grandma doesn't like you in elevators.

Laurie: I don't like me in elevators.

Theresa: Ha! That's why! Can I tell you something? Your grandmother is extremely strong.

Laurie: Oh yeah.

Theresa: Who's the JR? Or the initials JR?

Laurie: His name is J.?

Theresa: Who?

Laurie: John R███████████. She used to take care of him.

Theresa: She's asking you to tell me the story about him.

Laurie: She married a man and had a baby by him.

Theresa: She did? And his name is?

Laurie: JR.

Theresa: How old is he?

Laurie: He just turned two. She died in February. My other aunt, that lives with her and used to take care of her, he used to see her every day.

Theresa: JR. He can see your grandmother. It's almost like the dog. But your grandmother didn't have this baby. It's her daughter's grandson.

Laurie: Yes.

Theresa: Oh okay. Her daughter's grandson. She wants you to know I hang out with him.

Laurie: I can see it.

Theresa: I think he's going to be creative, this child. He's either going to be musical, or creative. There's something different about him.

Laurie: Yeah. You can tell that.

Theresa: If you were to give him colors to draw, pay attention to the colors he uses. You will see his creativeness in his coloring. Grandma is now showing me the supermarket that recently went out of business.

Laurie: The store?

Theresa: Did somebody work at a food store? Was there a ████████ nearby?

Laurie: Her daughter, JR's grandmother, works at a food store.

Theresa: Oh okay. She calls it the ████████.

Laurie: Yeah, that's her thing.

Theresa: She doesn't like that store.

Laurie: She doesn't like it. Even when she was alive, she was very vocal about how much she didn't like it.

Theresa: Oh really. She still doesn't like it, she's saying. Do you pray?

Laurie: Um. No. Not really.

Theresa: Do you have a belief in a higher being?

Laurie: Yeah.

Theresa: I ask because it's so easy for them to come to you. And they are all around you. Your grandmother almost lives with you! And she's doing what she needs to do on the other side as well. She's saying, don't let people tell you that if I stay with you I'm not resting in peace. I did my time on earth, but this is what I choose to do. I want to be near my loved ones. I still do what I have to do for God. She shows me a little pony. Who has a picture, either on a little horse or of a little horse? Oh my God! No! I know what this means! I did have this dream, last night, with two ponies. She's telling me that she sent me this dream. The meaning can be for me or someone else. Wow! It's amazing what she just did. I can only appreciate this now because I can remember the dream. Grandma had these two ponies coming down a driveway. They were black and they were small Shetland ponies. They were both black and they were beautiful. Black isn't indicative of...

Laurie: The dark side.

Theresa: Yes. So don't worry about it.

Laurie: Black's my favorite color.

Theresa: But she is talking about the pony. Now, does mom have a picture on a horse or near a horse when she was young?

Laurie: I don't know. I haven't seen it.

Theresa: This is going to be the "Aha" moment. There's usually at least one during a reading. The meaning will become clear to you when you're not thinking about it. The meaning just pops into your head. So let it go for now. Why is grandma bringing me with you all the way upstate?

Laurie: I travel to Connecticut.

Theresa: Okay. That's why. Who do you know with a criminal past?

Laurie: ███████████ is the only person that would pop in my head. And my sister's boyfriend ███████████, actually too.

Theresa: Grandma's not too crazy about the boyfriend.

Laurie: No one is.

Theresa: Oh okay. Do something. Not you, but she's talking to your mother and she's talking to your father. Do something about it.

Laurie: Oh yeah, they're trying.

Theresa: She's going to try too because he has a bad influence on your sister. Her pot is going to hurt her because it will lead to heavier drugs if something isn't done. Okay? Now Grandma is making me very dizzy and very nauseous. Who either had the flu, or I was always nauseous. Now nauseous for me can also mean cancer but your grandmother's saying no. It's like there's something inside me eating me up.

Laurie: No one was sick.

Theresa: Okay. Ask your mother about her grandmother.

Laurie: Oh wow.

Theresa: Because your grandmother is bringing in someone else. She stands right near your grandmother.

Laurie: A direct grandmother?

Theresa: It could be. That's the type of energy.

Laurie: My grandfather's mother just passed away.

Theresa: Do you know what she passed of?

Laurie: She was old. That's all I could tell you. I have no idea.

Theresa: I'm going to tell you, this woman was nauseous. I feel the life being drained out of me and I was so ready to go when it happened. Please keep this in mind. They keep bugging me with August. So let's do August. It's either August, the eighth of any month or the number eight.

Laurie: There's someone whose birthday is August eighth.

Theresa: Who's this?

Laurie: Three of my cousins and my uncle.

Theresa: One of the three has movement near them. Movement is a good thing.

Laurie: Is it marriage?

Theresa: I don't know but it could be. Grandma is happy about that. You're going to have stomach issues. Either the food doesn't agree with you or you have a weak stomach.

Laurie: Going to have or have?

Theresa: You could have it if it's recent.

Laurie: I don't eat since my stomach surgery. It's a sleeve to lose weight.

Theresa: Oh okay. That's a stomach issue. The number two big time. So let's go. February, the second of any month or the number two.

Laurie: She passed in February.

Theresa: Yeah, but this is something else. We acknowledged that she passed in February. She's not going to repeat herself.

Laurie: Her brother passed away.

Theresa: That's how she brings her brother in to be acknowledged. Who had the fake teeth or I'm having teeth problems? Two things, she's going near your mom and near your house.

Laurie: My aunt. Her daughter.

Theresa: Who's ███?

Laurie: She's the one who's August eighth.

Theresa: Wow! Your grandmother is giving me great confirmations. Now she's showing me words. That could mean crossword puzzles. I'm very good with words. There's something with words.

Laurie: Does it have to be a good thing?

Theresa: It could be whatever. It's your gut feeling.

Laurie: My aunt talks a lot. She uses words to hurt people.

Theresa: Your grandmother says, "they'll learn." Do you have a house that you live in?

Laurie: An apartment.

Theresa: Okay. But do you own the yard?

Laurie: I don't own the building. My grandpa does.

Theresa: I can go there because Grandma makes me feel ownership. That's why I thought it was a house. So you do have access to the yard.

Laurie: Yeah.

Theresa: Okay. She wants a bird feeder.

Laurie: Oh Jesus. She would.

Theresa: That's why it's the bird eggs. See I may not get the meaning of a sign in the beginning of a read so sometimes they lead me around. It's like they put a ring in my nose and they lead me to where I need to go. This is a process and it proves that there isn't any fakeness here. Grandma mentions something about a warranty on the car. Who helped you buy this car?

Laurie: My sister helped me lease it.

Theresa: Oh it's a lease. Alright. She's talking warranty, but maybe she means the lease. Did you read the lease well?

Laurie: No.

Theresa: Okay. Read the lease. You don't drive much, do you?

Laurie: Correct.

Theresa: Grandma wants to remind you that you only get a certain amount of mileage. So keep an eye on that.

Laurie: Okay.

Theresa: You're not supposed to take aspirin.

Laurie: Yeah.

Theresa: Oh you know that?

Laurie: Yeah. I had an allergic reaction to it once and never took it again.

Theresa: Another great sign!

Laurie: Yeah. No one knows that. No one knows about it.

Theresa: Oh okay. But your grandmother does know. Now, it would be curious for me to know, did she know about it when she was in body form?

Laurie: No.

Theresa: Can she prove herself any more than what she has already? She adores you. She's putting her money on you, she says. You're the one that's going to make a difference. You're the one. But there's a lot of heartache. She's saying, try not to miss me so much. Just look around for me. I'm around. I'm around. Now I see balloons. Is there a kids party coming up?

Laurie: Possibly.

Theresa: She wouldn't show me a possible. Balloons. Is someone getting married? There are balloons. I'm in celebration of something.

Laurie: Her son's son is getting married.

Theresa: When's he getting married?

Laurie: The fourteenth.

Theresa: Of?

Laurie: November.

Theresa: Oh, okay. I can go there. And something about a ballot. Do you not vote?

Laurie: I vote.

Theresa: Keep voting, she said because the other ones are lazy. Keep voting because it does makes a difference. I don't even know if grandma voted. Did you know her gums hurt her?

Laurie: No.

Theresa: Her mouth was hurting her.

Laurie: My grandma?

Theresa: Yeah. They're achy. Obviously not in excruciating pain, but they were achy. Grandma thought 'Oh my God even my gums! Even my gums hurt'. Grandma puts the initial "V" near you. Who is this person?

Laurie: The only "V" I know is V█████████.

Theresa: And who is that?

Laurie: That's a friend of mine.

Theresa: No. It's not him. She saying he's on the other side. 'The Italian' is with me. That's how I know you're not Italian.

Laurie: The Italians owned the building.

Theresa: She's referring to them as "Italians?"

Laurie: That was the way she always approached them. Never by name.

Theresa: So Grandma is showing me one of her personality traits. Remember they have to constantly prove it's them. Someone is going to go in for an EKG. (Electrocardiogram: to check the heart) They're going to find just a little something. But it's a good thing that it was found. She doesn't even think medication is going to be needed.

Laurie: Okay.

Theresa: Grandma goes near the twenty-sixth of a month. So it could be twenty-fifth, twenty-sixth, or twenty-seventh. It's not a holiday. They don't give me holidays. Did anything happen around the twenty-sixth of the month? Did anybody pass around the twenty-fifth, twenty-sixth, twenty-seventh of a month?

Laurie: This year? There were a lot of them.

Theresa: Your grandmother's bringing in this person and I believe it's male, not female.

Laurie: Her brother maybe. He died four weeks after she did.

Theresa: His birthday could have been around the twenty-sixth of the month. His passing could have been around the twenty-sixth of a month. You do bring in a lot of people. I see a long car so this is a limo. Other than the wedding, because they already acknowledge the wedding, either someone is renting out a limo or using a cab service to go somewhere. I'm either going to the airport in a hired car. Why is Grandma showing me this?

Laurie: I have no idea if it's a limo?

Theresa: It can be a cab service as well. I get the feeling that I am either going to an airport or down to New York City.

Laurie: Well tonight I'm going to the city. For the holiday.

Theresa: Your grandmother will be tagging along with you.

Laurie: Jesus!

Theresa: Watch where you bring her to, she's saying. Grandma stands on your left side because she's your heart, she says, and because you are hers. She will be talking to you a lot. Remember when they talk to us it feels like a gut feeling. Ask her to do something specific for you when you are alone and she'll do it. She won't appear. That really will frighten you.

Laurie: Yeah.

Theresa: Yeah that's what she said. That's not her thing. You did well. I'm glad you came.

Laurie: I'm glad I came too.

Theresa: Grandma makes me feel that there was some hesitancy you were feeling.

Laurie: Yes. Because it's Halloween and that's scary.

Theresa: Oh okay.

Laurie: It was a scary thought.

Theresa: Well now you can replace that feeling and substitute it with the memory of grandma coming through to talk with you on October thirty-first.

Laurie: Yeah on Halloween!

Chapter 3

FEAR OF THE LADY

I was eight years old, turning nine, when my family moved out of the Bronx and into the suburbs of Yonkers. This was back in the sixties. Yonkers wasn't anything like the bustling city it is today. This was a huge change for me. It was like I walked out of the city and into the country.

It was so quiet upstate. Up here was silence. And crickets. In the Bronx we lived directly across the street from a firehouse. I was used to sirens and radios and pissed off drivers honking their horns while screaming obscenities' waving one finger salutes. And the noise wasn't the only thing missing.

There were no stores. I was used to corner stores and pizza parlors, delis and bowling alleys all within walking distance. That's how it was in the Bronx. If you needed it or wanted it it was only a few blocks away. Yonkers was a whole new life. The streets in Yonkers were narrow and lined with single-family homes. Not a single store for miles. How can people live like that? What do you do when you need something? Plan a day trip? Take a personal day from work? Well, I suppose you could ask a neighbor if it was something important. There were plenty. Plenty of rows and rows of single-family houses that went on and on and on until it reached a forest.

Thankfully, we got out of the country often and I got to tell these stories to all my city friends when we visited. My entire family still lived in the Bronx so we traveled down there pretty consistently and definitely during the holidays.

I don't remember what Easter it was, but there was snow on the ground that year. Dad lifted each of us kids, one by one, out of the car and over the snow to the sidewalk. The entire family piled into the basement of my grandmother's house. Just like the attic, the basement ran almost the entire length of the building making it the only place where the whole family would fit. Well, there was one more place; a two-car garage, but we reserved that for nicer days.

In a typical Italian family, the kitchen of the matriarch is the hub of the family. When we lived there, I'd have to go down one flight of stairs from my third-floor apartment to the second floor of my grandmother's level. That's where her bedrooms were. I never saw my grandmother go to church, but she incorporated her love for God and the Saints in her everyday life. She even had an altar in her bedroom. I saw it once.

I lived there for nine years and only spent one night in my grandmother's room. I tried sleeping with her in her bed, but during the night my grandmother called my mother to come downstairs to get me because she thought I was possessed. Apparently, I used to speak in another language while sleeping. Apparently I also moved around a lot. That was the last time I was allowed to sleep downstairs.

On that same floor was her summer kitchen. No one ever cooked in the summer kitchen. Then there was a gated living room that had my Aunt Tessie's belongings in it. The room was only opened for wedding pictures and then closed again with strict rules never to enter. After the living room was the last set of stairs leading to the ground floor. The downstairs room had a couch, a bar, television and the kitchen where all entertaining took place.

A Roman Catholic Italian Easter meal is a grand event. They can easily last six hours or so, courses being served every so often. Between courses the kids would run off to play. The adults would sit around the table enjoying cigarettes and good conversation. I did neither. I was the eldest of grandma's thirteen grandchildren so I let the kids be kids, the adults be adults, and although I considered myself an "adult" I planned on being grandma's helper. I said goodbye to the kids outside and headed to the kitchen.

The entrance to the basement consisted of two separate doors - one in the back of the house and one on the side. Either door would you lead into the kitchen. My family, although devout, were somewhat superstitious. The house rule was if you enter through a door, you must exit through the same door. If you didn't, you ran the risk of bad luck. I entered through my "safe" door and found grandma in her housecoat sitting in her green recliner with her leg up on her ottoman. Grandma always wore a housecoat. Easter was no exception. She was nursing a case of gout - a type of arthritis. The television had on an Easter movie and the house smelled like roasting lamb and simmering gravy. I kissed her hello and turned to see what she was watching.

A wedding scene showed a beautiful light brown haired bride standing next to her handsome groom. She reminded me of the Lady in White! The ceremony was outside on what appeared to be a beautiful day. Standing next to the groom was his little girl with bouncy baby curls and sweet little dimples. She couldn't have been much older than four. The couple

"I do'd" and the little girl starts jumping up and down, squealing how happy she is to have a new mommy. She runs towards the bride for a hug. The bride bends down to embrace the child.

The camera moves to show the little girl from behind. You can't see the bride's face anymore. Just her hands. One of them was on the little girl's back. The other hand cupped the back of the little girl's head. That's when I noticed the woman's nails for the first time. They were quite long. Almost unnaturally long. The tips of them ended in a point. A sharp point. She curled her fingers into the back of that little girl's head. I knew she wanted to hurt her. She wanted to dig those nails deep into that little girl's head. She wanted to harm her. Suddenly the woman on screen was the Lady in White - my friend since birth. But I'd never seen her like this. She was always so nice. On TV she was menacing. I doubted her. For the first time in my life, I was afraid of the Lady in White.

I looked over at my grandmother who immediately blurted out, "Please don't be afraid to go back into the attic!"

She knew! She knew about the Lady in White! Why else would she say that?

"No." I shook my head while it all sank in. "No. No!"

Grandma softly grabbed me by the shoulder to stop me from walking away. "She would never hurt you. She's your Aunt!"

"My Aunt?"

"Yes. She's your Aunt Tessie." Grandma cried out with tears in her eyes. "She passed away two months before you were born. You were named after her."

I jerked away from Grandma. I couldn't take it anymore. My head was about to explode. I ran through my safe door and outside to be alone and absorb this new information. The Lady in White, the woman that basically raised me was actual blood! Today, for the first time, I saw her almost draw someone else's. I saw what she was capable of. After that day I never stepped foot in the attic or saw the Lady in White again.

Or should I call her Aunt Tessie now? Dear old Aunt Tessie who died too young two months before I was born. Dear old Aunt Tessie (Tessie was short for Theresa) who was laid to rest in her wedding dress. It was a beautiful long white dress. (I didn't find that out until I was in my forties).

Chapter 3 ½
HEATHER'S READING
A TESTIMONIAL

My name is Heather. I was a thirty-year-old single mother who was still too scared to go in the attic by herself when I met Theresa. I'd taken a job at a marble and granite fabricator and she was a friend of the boss' wife, Amy. It was a small family-run business with only a handful of people on payroll. The husband and wife ran the company and their niece, Lisa ran the office. I was only a few weeks in and barely knew anything about them. Theresa had come in once or twice to visit Amy and Lisa had mentioned she was a psychic. She said she did readings with a pencil. I was intrigued.

But it was more than that. There was a feeling I got when Theresa came in that was electric. Something about her felt familiar, like family. A little voice in my head kept repeating to me that this woman had the answer to questions I've had about my own spirituality. I just needed to ask her.

A conference table in the middle of the showroom served as our lunch spot and meeting place. I sat next to Lisa and across from Theresa, patiently waiting for the magic to begin.

I watched Theresa hand Lisa a pencil and told her to rub her energy on it. A few quick rubs across her palm and the pencil was passed back to Theresa. Theresa put the pencil against the paper and started to draw circles and random lines.

Theresa said a few things that were meaningless to me, not knowing Lisa all too well. Then she grabbed onto her stomach and moaned.

"Someone close to you is having surgery on their stomach and you're worried."

Lisa's phone started ringing in her pocket. Without missing a beat Theresa pointed to the phone. "And it's the person calling you right now."

Lisa pulled the phone out of her pocket and looked at the caller id. "It's my sister. Her surgery is this Friday."

I sat at that table, completely lost for words and thought to myself, 'Wow. This woman is legit.' Followed by 'I really, really, really want a reading.' But since I didn't know her, I kept my mouth shut and never said a word. I silently became a fan.

Although she was very polite when she came to visit, we didn't talk much, other than hello and goodbye before and after she entered Amy's office. And when Amy and her got together, it was doors closed. But since my desk was right outside, and both these ladies are Italian, it was easy to hear them through the door.

Amy was into tarot card readings and although Theresa preferred other means, she would allow Amy to practice with her, offering an interpretation once in a while. I know most people would find this kind of office atmosphere unusual - maybe be freaked out a bit. But I'm not like most people, nor was I raised to be what society would consider "normal".

I could give you a million reasons why, but here's just one thing about me most people consider unconventional. I'm a child of the eighties. Both of my parents were confirmed Christians - my mother Catholic and my father Episcopalian, or as he often referred to it "Christian-lite". Although my parents spent their childhoods attending CCD classes and confessing their sins, they decided against it for their own children. My sister and I were given a choice. We were able to choose our own religions. And if I didn't like my choices, I was allowed to make up my own. Which I did.

I remember attending my first funeral at a very young age. A lady in a long black dress stood across the way as I held my mother's hand. I felt horrible because I had no other emotion for my deceased relative whom I'd never met. It was the lady in the black dress that made me tear up. She sobbed uncontrollably, taking every few seconds to lift her head out of her palms to gasp for air. She was suffocating, drowning in sorrow and it broke my young heart.

When I was eleven years old, my twelve-year-old cousin lost her battle with Cystic Fibrosis. This time it was different. This time I stood on the hillside and became the lady in the black dress.

It's hard to handle death at any age. My way of handling it was to be baptized, just in case. I just needed a holy person to bless me. My sister decided to join me so we picked godparents and found a church that was willing to perform the ceremony without us having to attend a single class. A donation and a few days later I walked into the church. I was fourteen years old wearing all black; dress, skirt, stockings, shoes. The face the priest made when he discovered this was all my idea was hysterical. I'm sure he had me pegged as a rebellious, gothic, atheist. None of which were true. Black has always been my color choice when it came to clothes.

The deed was done. I was baptized which, according to the priest, wiped away all my sin and I started fresh. Imagine that, a clean slate from God and parents willing to allow me to choose how to worship God.

I spent the rest of my years researching, reading, and more importantly experiencing different walks of faith to determine my own path. I've attended different churches, my father's always being my favorite. I've attended synagogues, monasteries and all things in between. I had been to psychics, witnessed sanitarian festivals and had my cards and palms read. I didn't settle on just one, I took bits and pieces of them all and put it together as my own. But boy did I still have a lot of questions.

Finally, that fateful day arrived. I sat at my desk on another mundane day at work. A tingle fired up both my arms and the surrounding air carried with it the same sensation. The door opened from the outside world and in walked Theresa - well dressed, perfect makeup, and a warm wash of energy. My heart skipped a beat. Anyone who's ever been star-struck would understand how I hard it was to concentrate on forming actual words. She greeted me with a "Hello" and a smile.

"Hey, Theresa. Amy's not in today."

"I didn't come here to see Amy." she smiled. "I came here to see you."

My heart almost popped out of my chest. Here it finally was. Theresa, the Medium, wanted to talk to me!

"There are flies around you."

I looked up towards the ceiling. This place wasn't the cleanest, but I hadn't noticed any buzzing or swatted anything off my coffee.

"Metaphysical flies," she smiled. "It means there's crap around you. And it's right at your front door. Picture your house as a step, and the next step is outside, but you can't leave because there it is, right at your doorstep. And the flies are buzzing around it, just waiting. In order to move forward, you have to deal with the crap."

I sat, jaw-open, head-racing, imagination about to explode. Somehow I managed to ask, "Well what the heck does that mean?".

Theresa just smiled. "That means it's time for me to give you a reading."

The next thing I know I'm sitting across from her in Lisa's office, door closed, rubbing a pencil between my hands - a method used to transfer one's energy to the item the reader will be reading.

I handed it back to her and she began to draw quick wide circles all over the paper. This was something I had done quite often since childhood. My mother taught me to look away from the paper and draw circles everywhere, then look at the paper and see if you could find a picture within the lines. I was excited to see this done in the form of a spiritual reading and waited for Theresa to fill up the paper. Instead, with only three small circles drawn out - certainly not enough to find an even halfway decent picture - she looked at me with a smirk. "Wow, you're thirty years old and still scared of the dark."

"You can see that!" Scared wasn't the word for what I was in the dark. I used to make my grandmother walk up three flights of stairs when I needed to get something down from the attic. I had perfected the art of wrapping my wrist around the corner of a wall to find the light switch on the other side before entering the room. I wasn't afraid. I was terrified.

"You have a third eye. But you already know that. Somehow, however, you have it closed. You chose to shut it down on purpose, but sometimes things trickle through. Sometimes you catch a glimpse of something - and it happens real quick - of an arm, or a person, or a shadow. You know you see it but you doubt yourself and tell yourself it's all in your imagination. But then you want to believe it, but you don't know what to believe."

I nodded, just barely and only once. I sat across from her, refusing to say anything that might "give something away" should she have been cold-reading. Cold-reading is a series of techniques used by scam artists to make them appear like they know more about you than they should. Cold Readers also look for clues in your body language, so I sat as still and emotionless as I could - given the excitement.

Theresa sat back and looked me dead in the eye. "Well, what if I told you that everything you were taught was just your imagination, was real?"

"What do you mean?"

She looked at me matter-of-factly. "You know you're a witch, right?"

"I always wanted to be a witch, since I was a kid," I chuckled.

"What little girl dreams of being a witch?" Theresa looked flabbergasted. "A princess, I understand. But a witch?"

"I'm an unusual girl," I replied. By now the pencil had gone cold and it was returned to me for a bit more rubbing to transfer my energy back into it.

I handed it back and watched more circles appear on the paper. So far, she had hit the nail on the head. Pretty good reading so far, considering I'd been exposed to several at this point in my life. But what she said next blew my mind and shattered everything I thought I understood into a million pieces.

"You know that dream you always have? The one where you're running through the forest with a group of people, there's a blond guy that jumps in front of your path and a Jamaican lady to your right. You know you're hunting something, but you don't know what it is."

I knew exactly what she was talking about. I've had that dream for so long that I first told my mother about it when I was about seven or so.

She continued. "And sometimes, when you wake up afterward, you think you see a little girl in a white dress, with black polka dots, blue eyes and long black hair. She reminds you of a doll that your grandmother gave you as a child. Looks just like her, bonnet and all."

I'd told my mother about that little girl. I can still remember crawling into her bed at 2 am because she scared me. This is normally when most parents give their kids the "it's all in your imagination" speech. Not in my house. My mom told me it was probably a ghost and not all ghosts are good so don't talk to it because then it can follow me. Then she gave me a kiss on the forehead and sent me back to bed. This just added to the list of reasons why I was absolutely fine sharing my bed with my eighty pound dalmatian and an old alley cat that attacked anything that moved, including feet.

She went on to explain that those that ran with me were my protectors. She mentioned I'd shared visits with them in other dreams as well. I knew that to be true. I have an insane ability to remember my dreams. I could tell you nightmares I had in kindergarten.

"I don't know what you did in your last life," Theresa said, "but for some reason, you got one heck of an army. And whatever crap there was is at your doorstep, you have to deal with it before you can move forward. Are you writing a book? You know you're going to be published one day."

I almost said something, but Theresa cut me off and said, "Not the one about the monkey". I was a bit taken back as I thought of my endless hours spent writing that book, editing, illustrating, not liking it and illustrating again. I dreamt of the day it sold. Now my dreams were slightly crushed but I wouldn't let this deter me. This was proof there was no way she could be cold reading.

She went on to explain a few odds and ends, each in vivid detail and absolutely true. I continued to sit stone-faced and listened intently.

"You have a third eye," Theresa said. "Somehow you scared it closed. But it doesn't want to be closed anymore. It's going to open whether you like it or not. That's why I was drawn to you. That's why I was meant to come in today and Amy wasn't meant to be here. Nothing in life is a coincidence. You'll understand that soon. Because I'm going to help you understand what's happening is okay. You don't need to be afraid of it. You just need to learn how to control it. If you believe in the light it can't harm you. You have no reason to be afraid."

When the reading what over I was a bundle of questions. We chatted for a while about everything and anything and got on the subject of Theresa's religious beliefs. As a Roman Catholic Medium, Theresa didn't exist in her own religion but was secretly sought out by other Christians and people of faith for her gifts. "If I had a dollar for every reading that ended with the person telling me, 'It's such a shame. You're a really great person. Your reading gave me so much closure and took such a heavyweight off my shoulders. But you're going to hell for being able to do this."

I couldn't help but laugh out loud. "So they basically tell you, you're a good person, but you're going to hell? Well, I refuse to believe that. But then again, I don't believe in "hell". I believe in reincarnation."

"Me too," Theresa replied. "But to each their own."

Chapter 4

SISTER "NOW NOW"

I turned off my gift Easter 1963, but I never turned away from God. By the time I was nine I'd already learned to interact with spirits and had grown to be a spiritual person, but I had no real concept of "religion" until I started catechism class.

Catechism class, or CCD as it's called nowadays, is a Catholic requirement. If you're Catholic and you don't go to an actual Catholic school, you're required to attend CCD classes to study the bible and the meaning of the gospel. Every Wednesday all the Catholic kids in my grade were dismissed a little earlier than the rest of the kids. We were escorted to our local parish to start our studies. Without them we wouldn't be able to receive any further sacraments required after your first holy communion and before your last rites. Marriage was on the list - meaning no CCD meant you wouldn't be allowed to marry, so I considered class very important.

There was something about being in class that felt like home. There was a knowing inside me. When I saw the Lady in White and when I spoke to the Virgin Mary it wasn't religious, it wasn't spiritual, it was just part of my world. Before I feared my Aunt when we used to speak there were no lessons attached. Just normal conversation like you'd have with a friend. The

Blessed Mother always postponed my lessons and refused to answer my questions until I'd be old enough to understand. But I knew that She loved me. She told me all the time. I knew that God loved me. I could feel it in my heart. Being afraid of my Aunt didn't change the way I felt about God. As a matter of fact it made me even more protective of Him. And I did not like the way Sister "Now Now" described him.

Sister "Now Now" was the name I gave to the CCD teacher that taught classes every Wednesday afternoon. She got that nickname from the way she constantly cut me off whenever I raised my hand.

"Now now Theresa. Let someone else speak."

But I had to raise my hand - most of the time. I hated the way she explained God. She made him seem mean and unloving. The way she enforced 'be fearful, don't sin, or you are going to hell school of thought.'

See what I mean? That wasn't the God I knew. My God wasn't anything like that. He loved me. I knew it. I could feel it in my heart and it physically hurt me to hear Him spoken about like that.

One time Sister "Now Now" taught us a lesson about Hell. She said if we didn't go to church you were making a mortal sin. If you sinned, then God was going to make you 'burn in the fiery pits of hell for all eternity'.

I raised my hand and started talking the moment she made eye contact. "I don't believe there's a place like that."

Sister "Now Now" rolled her eyes and crossed her arms against her chest. "And why not?"

"Because that would make my dad better than God. See, no matter what I did my father would never ever kick me out of his house for good. Even if I lied to him. Even if I stole money from his pocket. He would never throw me out of his house - especially for all eternity. God loves me, so He wouldn't do that either or else that would make my dad better than God. And no one is supposed to be better than God."

"Now now Theresa," she shook her head. "Let someone else speak." She quickly changed the subject, called out a random question and pointed to a girl in the front row.

It was like I could feel my heart break in half to hear Him spoken about like that. Sister "Now Now" was wrong. Completely wrong. My God wasn't like that. My God still loved me even though I've personally sinned.

I snuck out of my house once. Left without permission. Disobeyed my parents' rules. But I knew God still loved me. See, my Dad's friend Larry came to visit with his wife and four sons. I saw that his right arm was at least three times larger than the left. Mom shushed the kids downstairs to play. I stood behind a door so they didn't see me and listened to them talk. I heard them say they "arrested the growing cancer and isolated it". That's what was wrong with Larry. Larry had cancer.

I didn't waste a moment. I went downstairs, out the basement door, and walked three miles to church. As soon as I got there I opened the door, walked inside, chose a pew, dropped to my knees and began praying for Larry and his sons.

I started off with the "Our Father". Then I asked God to please help Larry's wife and kids be okay. My intuition told me what Larry had was a death sentence. I prayed he wouldn't suffer too much. I asked God to help his wife and kids heal and find happiness again after Larry was gone. I asked God to please make sure my parents stayed healthy. Last but not least, I asked God for forgiveness and to please make it so I didn't get caught or in too much trouble for sneaking out.

I went back home the same way I originally came - through my safe door and back to my room. No one noticed I'd been gone. God works in mysterious ways and He listens to prayers even if you have to break the rules in order to be heard. Larry did end up passing away. We never saw his family again, but I knew all of them would be fine and Larry would be watching over them.

I received my first communion twice. In the Catholic faith, receiving your first communion is a monumental event which must be earned. Part of earning was learning. One of our CCD lessons was to participate during nine o'clock mass when they announced it was time to receive communion. We were told get in line with the rest of the congregation, but this was a dry run for us. The priest knew we were just practicing walking through the line. He was supposed to skip us. He wasn't supposed to offer us the communion bread. We hadn't earned the right to receive it yet. But for some reason, when I got up there, the priest offered me communion.

There I was, six years old, God in my heart and the Virgin Mother in my backyard in front of a priest who was offering me communion bread. Who was I to tell him no? He was a priest. I smiled and quickly put the offering in my mouth. Now came the hard part everyone always talked about. You're not supposed to chew it. You're supposed to let it dissolve in your mouth. Problem was, mine wasn't dissolving. I dug at the roof of my mouth with my tongue and mushed it around as much as I could without teeth.

Some people in the pews must have recognized what I was doing because by the time we got back home our telephone was on fire. It seemed the whole neighborhood was calling to rip my mom apart about what a heathen I was. How dare I take communion when I wasn't supposed to!

I told my mom the same thing I had told myself. He was a priest. I wasn't going to tell him no. Once mom calmed down a bit, I asked her if she could take my picture while I stood outside next to the Virgin Mother.

A short while later I received my second first communion with my classmates as planned; all dolled up in my communion dress and fancy shoes. Looking back, I really believe it was supposed to happen this way.

After my second first communion I practically lived in my special shoes. They were filthy. A year later my little sister was to receive her first communion. After her church service my mother had me put on my communion clothes to take a picture next to the Virgin Mother. She had me stand on one side of Our Lady and my sister on the other. My sister's dress and shoes were in pristine condition. I had on dirty shoes. I hated those shoes and didn't want to stand next to the Virgin Mother dirty. But I did and I resigned myself to the thought of my humiliation being a consequence of taking the communion bread a week before my First Holy Communion.

I would have made a great nun. Or so I thought when I was nine. I told my priest. He he told to me to wait until I was older to make that decision.

"If you still want to be a nun when you're sixteen, come talk to me," was his reply.

That's when I really started to question religion. Why would he think I would change my mind as I got older? What would I learn that could turn me around? I wanted to know, so I continued to study.

The more I learned about religion the more questions I had. I was getting comfortable with the other side, in a spiritual way, not just with spirits. There was a knowing inside of me, about God, about how much He loved me. About the Virgin Mother and how much She loved me. They didn't care that I messed up sometimes. They knew I meant well.

Between nine and sixteen, I was more connected to my beliefs as a Christian and not a "practicing" medium. Once I'd made a decision to shut off my gift - the day the Lady in White appeared on TV - the Spirits as well as my guides, respected my decision. They came for higher purposes. They came from the light. When I decided to shut off my gift, they graciously left me alone like I asked and patiently waited for me to return.

It was my decision to turn off my gift. It stayed off for nearly seven years before I was abruptly reintroduced to the spirit world by way of a very evil energy. My first introduction to the spirit world was through light and love. My return was through dark and hatred. I learned where there is good, there is bad. It's the only way to keep balanced.

Chapter 4 ½

LYNN'S READING

Lynn: I am so nervous.

Theresa: Just try to relax. This really is a very simple process. Ready?

Lynn: I guess.

Theresa: Your grandfather is coming in. He's making my back hurt. He says that back problems run in your family. Does this make sense to you?

Lynn: Yes. Do you know what grandfather this is?

Theresa: He mentions the name Fran, Francis, Frank.

Lynn: That's my grandfather Frank.

Theresa: He's bringing in horses.

Lynn: Why?

Theresa: The spirits speak to me in my language - symbolisms. When I see a horse it can mean literally, maybe someone owns or rides horses, or they have a connection to Bronx, New York. I say that because when I was growing up in the Bronx there was a stable along the parkway.

Lynn: I'm sorry, but that doesn't make any sense to me.

Theresa: Okay. I'm trying to have your grandfather release this image from my mind, but he's refusing.

Lynn: Oh my! I really can't connect this.

Theresa: I'm starting to wonder why he isn't releasing me from this image. Please keep in mind that if it wasn't a memory, it might be a current event.

Lynn: I wonder if this means anything. Just the other day I was talking to my friend and she wanted to go to ██████████ Raceway.

Theresa: That's it! Make sure you go. Your grandfather is going to go with you.

Lynn: That doesn't surprise me. He loved betting on horses.

Theresa: Your grandfather makes me feel that his throat was his trauma area. Did he have throat cancer or a tube down his throat?

Lynn: He did have throat cancer and he had a trach.

Theresa: Of course you know he doesn't feel that discomfort any longer. He's only using that as a sign. Your grandfather is pointing to the other grandfather who is standing next to him. He brings in Archangel Michael. When I see Archangel Michael, it can mean any of the following; the name Michael means something to you, the month of September or the ninth of any month, someone is or was a police officer. Archangel Michael is the patron Saint of firemen and police officers.

Lynn: The name Michael means something to me. That would be one of his grandsons.

Theresa: He makes me feel there is more.

Lynn: I did know a police officer who has passed.

Theresa: No, he makes me feel something else. Does the ninth of any month mean something to you?

Lynn: Not off the top of my head.

Theresa: Okay. Well I'm not being released of this image.

Lynn: I think I know! His wife's birthday has always been questioned. We don't know if it's the ninth or the tenth of September.

Theresa: Tell your family it's the ninth. This grandfather is showing me an arrow through your heart. The initial injury to the heart happened years ago and the scarring is now taking place.

Lynn: Yes. My marriage started falling apart.

Theresa: Your grandfather wants to talk about the month of February. Is someone's birthday in February?

Lynn: Yes. My son.

Theresa: This grandfather is putting creativity near him.

Lynn: Yes.

Theresa: Your grandfather is starting to bring in another energy. My neck hurts, but it is connected to my heart. It's my carotid artery.

Lynn: Yes, that's the policeman!

Theresa: He is handing you roses. Does this make sense to you?

Lynn: Yes.

Theresa: He is trying to tell me that he was trying to get headphones on you.

Lynn: That's so funny you should say that. I was online and I was going to buy headphones but decided not to.

Theresa: Maybe you better purchase them. Your grandfather is telling me that this is the first time they're meeting.

Lynn: Yes.

Theresa: Your grandfather likes this person. I'm hearing the name Margaret or Margie. Can you acknowledge this?

Lynn: No. Not yet.

Theresa: They are showing me someone painting or doing renovations.

Lynn: Yes. My husband is in that line of work.

Theresa: Your grandfather just wrote "Staten Island" across my mind. Why?

Lynn: My cousin just moved there and it's his grandson.

Theresa: Okay. Please tell your cousin that the grandfather knows of the move and is wishing him well. The grandfather who showed up after Frank is more quiet and more subtle in his ways. He wants to tell you that he doesn't need to make big pronouncements. He was and is closer to you. Does this make sense to you?

Lynn: Yes.

Theresa: Your grandfather Frank is holding a cake and is getting ready for the celebration. Can you acknowledge this?

Lynn: Yes. We are celebrating my daughter's birthday this weekend.

Theresa: Please know that your grandfather will be there. They want to end this session by showing their love to the month of November. Does this make sense to you?

Lynn: Yes! It's my birthday.

Chapter 5

THE LEONA DRIVE DEVIL

It was a random Saturday morning in the spring of 1970. My sisters and I had consulted Mom's chore chart which left me elbows deep in the sink.

Mom kept her chart on the fridge. It cycled us girls through everything on a weekly basis. And when I say everything, I mean everything - laundry, washing the bathroom walls, cleaning the windows, polishing furniture, mopping the floors, doing the dishes - all laid out in list form right there on the fridge leaving no questions about who was responsible for what. There were also "meal" chores to be done every day. This included preparing dinner sometimes, setting and cleaning up the table and we were expected to keep our rooms clean at all times. My brother's only chore was taking out the trash (and he rarely did that) so he was exempt from the chore chart. That left me and four sisters to pick up the slack.

Usually, after chores, we went outside to play with our neighborhood friends. When I needed some me time I'd bring my pillow outside and catch up on some cloud watching. But today I didn't want to do anything like that. I was tired after cleaning - so much that I suddenly, desperately needed a nap so I went to my "room" to lay down.

I called it my "room" because it was really two couches in the basement. My couch was against the wall of the staircase that led up to our kitchen. My sisters was against the far wall. I plopped down on my couch and got comfortable. Upstairs I could hear my mother talking to her friend Fran and both women were loud. They weren't screaming or fighting - they were just two Italian women talking.

Great, I thought. *How am I supposed to fall asleep now?*

I got up and dragged my couch across the room where the sub pump was and laid back down. No good. I could still hear them. With nothing left to do I just closed my eyes and tried my best to ignore them.

There comes a point in every sleep cycle when your conscious and your subconscious meet. It's that moment when you consciously know you're falling into subconsciousness; you can feel yourself drifting away. I had just started to drift when I felt a sudden shift like the room itself was now askew. Something wasn't right.

Allow me to explain. I react to energy. I can feel it. Energy is everywhere so I feel it constantly. We all emit our own energies and they each feel a little different. Say I'm walking down the street and a little girl is walking towards me; I feel one type of energy. If two girls are walking towards me, the energy shifts because two different personalities are now on my path. However, this didn't feel like the energy of two little girls. This was a dark shift. A heavy shift. It made me nervous. I knew it had to be something bad. My hands started to tingle and sweat. I felt off balanced, yet very aware something was happening. Then came the fear. I was frozen. Petrified of whatever this was that caused this shift.

Mom was laughing upstairs with our neighbor Fran. They were going on and on about this one and that one in the neighborhood. Normal housewife gossip. By the sound of it, it was juicy. I focused on the sound of these two women talking. I paid close attention to their conversation and used it to secure my own energy to the earth plane.

This dark energy weighed me down. It felt like a giant boulder sat on my chest. Breathing started to get hard. The reflexive task of inhaling and exhaling was a struggle. When I did breathe in, I smelled death. I was enveloped by death. So I stopped breathing.

The energy pushed against my nostrils like it wanted to get inside. I held my breath, but it took it from me. Literally took my breath from me then gained control of my lungs. This was how it got inside. It made me breathe it in. It rode my breath into my body and took control. All five of my senses were useless; every muscle, every vein, every organ now inhibited by something vile and foreign. It had reduced me to its marionette. The ability to breathe on my own had completely disappeared. It forced me to inhale its pure evil.

My ankles began to tingle. A cold sensation worked its way toward my waist leaving a trail of shivers and fear. The tingling grew stronger when it got to my chest. It lingered there a while. Perhaps looking for my soul. The entire room grew ice cold. Every inch of me just as cold. Whatever this was drained the life out of me. I knew I was going to die. I closed my eyes and prepared to be with God.

That's when I heard more laughter. Bone-chilling, unearthly laughter. The kind that would leave a navy seal shaking in his or her boots. I couldn't help myself. My curiosity overshadowed my fear. I had to know what was laughing like that so I opened my eyes and looked around.

I could see the wall on the opposite side of my bed. Mom had hung a trio of facial plaques that depict various stages of laughter, sorrow, and surprise. I'd always hated those things, since the moment my mom decided to hang them there. I didn't like them then, and I definitely didn't like that them now that they were all facing me laughing. All three of them had turned to face me eye to eye and were laughing like the devil himself.

I couldn't let this happen. I wanted to crawl inside my body, through my veins and reach my soul before this being had its chance to conquer me. I knew that Jesus resided in my soul and could destroy this being with only a breath. This energy knew that too. It started moving towards my mouth. I couldn't scream. I couldn't move. And I couldn't breathe. It didn't want me to be able to cry out for help. The only sense it left me was hearing.

I could still hear Mom talking to Fran. The conversation sounded friendly, easy going. I didn't understand how they could be carrying on like that while I laid here fighting for my life. I needed help, and I needed it now.

That's when I heard the voice of the Virgin calling to me in Her sweet angelic way. She told me to grab onto my cross, the one that hung from my neck. She told me to grab onto it and pray. The moment I started to pray inside my head the energy disappeared. Just like that it released me and was gone. I felt my hand wipe the sweat from my face. I could move again.

I ran full speed upstairs to the kitchen. Mom and Fran were mid gossip still in the places I'd envisioned them when I heard them talking earlier. Though I felt like I'd been held down for much longer, the reality was only moments had passed. Time works different on the other side.

I needed to know if what happened to me was real or a nightmare. I needed to know if that energy was real. If what just happened really happened. Mom and Fran were talking about something while I was held down. Something adult. I asked my mom what it meant. Mom's face turned red, and I was in trouble for eavesdropping. It didn't matter to me though. I was too angry to care. I'd received validation. What I just experienced was very real. It was not my imagination.

I told my mother I was throwing out the plaques. I told her they frightened me. That was all she needed to know. She didn't need to know they frightened me because they had been possessed and laughed at me while something vile held me in a psychic struggle. There are a few things young girls needn't admit to our mothers and I believed my paranormal experiences fit into that category quite well.

Many years later my mother officially found out about my abilities. I was an adult and went to her house to visit. I told her, "Dad's here and he wants you to know he's happy you found the beads".

"How do you know that?" She asked and I explained.

"Well, you remember the Aunt Tessie thing?" However, we didn't speak about the plaques until I was in my fifties. That's when mom finally spilled the beans and filled me in on the missing piece of the puzzle. Or should I say an extra piece?

We were having a cup of coffee talking about me as a kid now that she knew about my gift. I told her I hated all three of those plaques since the day she put them on my wall.

"There were only two," Mom corrected.

"No. There were three. The happy, sad, and surprised."

"I'm telling you, Theresa," Mom insisted, "I bought them. I should know. There were only two. The happy and the sad. Look it up on the internet. They only sell those things in pairs of happy and sad."

I spent the next three weeks scouring the net looking for the three faces that haunted my past. And I never found them. Just pages and pages of pairs. I even found mom's pair. Apparently they were drama masks also known as Comedy, the happy one, and Tragedy, the sad one. There was no Surprise.

That's when mom admitted it. "It was probably the Ouija board I had in the attic, not the plaques". That one remark delivered so much. The hair on the back of my neck stood up. It answered questions I hadn't even thought to ask regarding my young paranormal experiences. It served as confirmation that all of what I'd experienced was real. It made me steadfast in my determination to deal with negative energies, whether my own or other people's, by using the power of prayer with no doubt and no fear.

That was the lesson the Virgin had waited to teach me! I sat next to Her, outside in the sun, snake at Her feet. Again, I asked Her if it hurt Her to stand on the snake. She answered inside my head.

"It doesn't hurt because I'm not afraid of it."

I told Her I didn't understand. She told me the snake was full of everyone's fears. That's how it grew to be so large. But She wasn't afraid of it because She believed in God, so the snake couldn't hurt Her.

"Evil can't get any higher than the bottom of your feet if you have no fear and believe in a higher being."

That night Aunt Tessie returned to me in my dreams. I wasn't afraid of her. She floated through the closed door, grabbed me by the hand and up we went. We flew through the city streets, navigating around the buildings with ease. Still higher we went until I could see all of Earth's mesmerizing glory. Still higher passed the man on the moon, passed endless rows of stars until we reached the heavens.

They were even more majestic than I could have imagined. A sprawling city of sorts, each building with a front door adorned with a crystal knob. Beautiful flowers unlike any I'd ever seen dotted along the grasslands. She brought me back to earth much like we'd come, but this time took me over the deserts on the way home. I'd never seen so much sand. Once I was safely back in bed, she smiled and disappeared.

My Aunt Tessie was letting me know it was okay to use my gifts again. The Virgin Mother taught me it would be okay too, as long as I never let the fear go higher than my feet.

Chapter 5 ½

JUDY'S READING

Theresa: I'm being told to mention the month of October. Please keep in mind it could mean the month of October, the tenth of any month, or the name Theresa or Terry. I can go there because, for me, this month is Saint Teresa's month. Or someone lived near a church. Now, I'm starting to get a headache.

Judy: I have some aspirin.

Theresa: No. It's not me who has the headache. It's someone from the other side making me feel head trauma. Or it can mean I either used to suffer with headaches when I was here in body form or someone does suffer with them. I have a female coming in. Older. Or I had a stroke or a blood clot where my head was the trauma area. Does that make sense to you?

Judy: I don't know. Nothing jumps out at me.

Theresa: I'm a grandmother type energy. I come in way above you.

Judy: Two grandmothers have passed.

Theresa: But I'm claiming you. When they claim you I go more towards the mother's mother because it's easier to claim the grandchild. And who's El, Ellen? It sounds like "EL". Something "EL". Now she's saying this. It doesn't have to be her name. It can be a nickname.

Judy: My husband has an Aunt ███████ they call Ellena.

Theresa: There you go. That's it. Ellena. It's the "El". She's going to have a message for this person. So this could be his grandma.

Judy: It's his family. See, I was very close to his family. We've been together a long time.

Theresa: Oh! Wait a minute. Is his grandmother on the other side? And her name is Ellena?

Judy: Her daughter's name we call Ellena.

Theresa: That's his grandmother. And she's claiming you because she was so close to you. Just so you know, she used to suffer with headaches. She comes and visits a lot. I don't know if I had, not Alzheimer's, but what's with her head?

Judy: Funny thing is, when she was finally sick at the end, she lived with Ellena. She had dementia. The end of her life was just that.

Theresa: There ya go. There's her head trauma. She had one foot there one foot here towards the end of her life. A lot of people thought she was confused.

The only time she was confused was when she opened her eyes, she said. When I opened my eyes and I was in my body form that's when the confusion hit me. Because I knew where I was during sleep. So why would she mention October, the tenth of any month or the number ten?

Judy: That's my anniversary. Ten, ten.

Theresa: That's why she's the one that reached out to me first with October because she had to confirm the wedding date. So she comes through love, but she comes in through your husband's family. Which became your family on October tenth. She also says, with October, to go to Saint Teresa. So, they're going to speak to me in my language, using my symbols. Keep that in mind. This is not going to be religious reading, but they do use spiritual signs for me. So either, someone's first, middle or last name was Theresa, or their chosen name, or someone lived near the church.

Judy: Well, living near a church makes more sense. I won't tell you the whole story, but I moved in next door to my husband's family; his grandmother and his mother lived there. This was right across from Sacred Heart Church.

Theresa: I'm going near the twenty sixth of a month. So it could be twenty-fifth, twenty-sixth, or twenty-seventh. Why? And this is the grandmother speaking.

Judy: I don't know when she passed. And I should know that date. The twenty-seventh is my husband's birthday. That's his number.

Theresa: She's very, very close to her grandson. This is now two times that she has reached out to him through you. They might not have been very close, because she shows me the energy is a little up and down, but right now she's very close to him. Now, there's a decision coming up he has to make. Who's Joe, or Joseph?

Judy: We have a Joe. My husbands brother. And his son's name is Joseph.

Theresa: She's reaching out to her family by name. She says, she can do this with you because you have more of a psychic nature.

Judy: I know.

Theresa: It's easy for you to speak for them.

Judy: Right. I have a lot of people tell me that. I'm sure a lot of people have that and they don't know that they have it.

Theresa: Who's ██████████?

Judy: Well...

Theresa: Gut feeling. It's always a gut feeling.

Judy: No, it's funny because of all the people to come through I would not think of her. There's a problem person in our family and that's her name. And she also lived here with everybody. She's just a problem person, you could call her.

Theresa: This grandmother is aware of what's going on. She shows me stirring the pot. So I don't know if ███████████ is stirring the pot.

Judy: She just has problems. We don't really know.

Theresa: Your grandmother knows and is aware of her energy.

Judy: *Laughs* There's a rift.

Theresa: She's going to try to help out with this situation. This grandmother.

Judy: Figures.

Theresa: I have another female coming through and I'm equal to you. So this is either a sister, a friend, a cousin or a coworker. And somehow the initial "P" is attached to it.

Judy: Equal like same age as me?

Theresa: Same generation. When they come in equal, it's the same generation. Did you have a coworker who passed?

Judy: You know, there was a woman that worked in the same place as me. Her name was Patty. That's so weird. Not that I didn't like her. I knew her but not really closely, like a little, you know?

Theresa: She has a sense of gratitude, attached to her, towards you. She makes me feel there used to be talk about her, but you were never part of it.

Judy: Yeah, I would never.

Theresa: So that's why she comes in. And she comes in because you have that psychic sign above you. You have the energy that it's easy.

Judy: Yeah, we discussed it. She was into this whole thing.

Theresa: There you go. So she's confirming.

Judy: You know how things come to you. Its weird. I did think of her recently because she did pass suddenly and it was just very upsetting.

Theresa: Do you remember what she passed of? Was it in the breast?

Judy: I think it was a heart attack. It was sudden, like one day she was planning for her daughter's bridal shower and the next Monday we were like 'what do you mean?'.

Theresa: Because she points to the breast, but maybe she meant heart attack. She's pointing to her breast. She's talking about the snow. She hates the snow. But to me there's a story attached to the snow with her. Or there was a story about snow at work. Or someone forced you to come in with the snow.

Judy: It's possible. I didn't know her well enough. It's possible.

Theresa: Okay. Remember earlier when I told you they're going to come in either with a current event or a memory. You were just currently thinking about her, so this was her current event.

Judy: Yeah.

Theresa: So let me explain how that works. I know that we feel like our gut feelings are our feelings, but they're not. We're being spoken to by the other side. But you were just thinking about her. The thought was yours but you were being encouraged by her. So it's not a coincidence she shows up. The other thing you have to keep in mind is when we deal with spirits on the other side we cannot use our brain. The minute we use our brain and try to make sense of it we're screwed. This is why we don't take the brain with us.

Judy: Right.

Theresa: Your TV; I have a father image on the other side near you. Explain him. Because he came in like a father energy.

Judy: My father-in-law. But very close. Very, very close.

Theresa: I don't pick up legalities of the relationship. Just the father type energy. So I'm coming down a lot, this father energy. He's saying two things. There's going to be something wrong with the TV. Either the TV is going to change itself or its going to go in and out. That's your father energy doing that. He's giving me permission for you to call him your father.

Judy: Yeah.

Theresa: Did anybody punch a wall? This could be a memory. Who had the short temper or who had an injury to their hands?

Judy: Nothing jumps out at me.

Theresa: What did your father-in-law do for a living?

Judy: He was a police officer.

Theresa: Which one of his survivors works with their hands? Or I think I'm a handyman.

Judy: Not one of his kids.

Theresa: He's showing me someone. Maybe someone got in a fight. There's a knuckle story.

Judy: I could ask. They're a very non fighting family.

Theresa: Unless it was this father himself.

Judy: I'll find out. You know when you don't think of it and then you're like, oh yeah remember that time.

Theresa: He's mentioning Lucie or Lucille. This is the letter "L". Not "EL" sound. I'm alive. I'm not passed. Do you know who he's speaking of?

Judy: Well he has a bunch of kids. He has one daughter named Lisa.

Theresa: That's the "L".

Judy: That's all I can think of.

Theresa: You always go with your gut feeling because that's them speaking to you. Then he's telling me there's something with her eyes. He makes me write "Lucy" because I'll go right away to... Oh, wait, I'm getting a heart attack.

Judy: I don't want to say anything. Please finish. Because it has to do with her. Not heart attack, but I don't want to give anything away. I don't want to influence your reading with her. But that makes sense if Lisa's the person.

Theresa starts getting a bit hoarse. Judy offers her a drink.

Theresa: No this is intuitive. But there's also something wrong with her eyes. She needs help, he's saying. And if I'm your father-in-law I know I can depend on you.

Judy: Yes you can. Oh my God! I'm her person. We joke around like that. You know, 'if something happens, you're my person'. We joke.

Theresa: He's not releasing me of the breast. Is she worried about breast cancer? What's going on?

Judy: Not that we know of, but there was an incident. She was having chest pains or whatever. See you went like that *points to breast* and said 'el'.

Theresa: Just so you know, it's going to be anxiety more than an actual heart problem.

Judy: That's what I'm thinking too.

Theresa: He's giving you the answer already.

Judy: I'll look out for her.

Theresa: I think he used to rub his chest a lot because he's making me rub mine. He knew more that he let on, he says. He had trouble breathing.

Judy: Yeah.

Theresa: He didn't want anybody worrying.

Judy: He had emphysema.

Theresa: So this is why. Either he knew longer than you guys knew or he knew more information than he was letting on. I didn't want to worry anyone. This was my thing. He's showing me a young boy on the other side. Who either had a miscarriage or lost a little boy?

Judy: I had a miscarriage before my children.

Theresa: This one was a boy and he's attaching the boy to you. Did you know the sex of the baby?

Judy: No.

Theresa: Alright so he's telling you it's a boy. He also wants me to mention the number eight. So I go either to August, the eighth of any month or the number eight.

Judy: Let me think. It wasn't his birthday. I think it was his mother's birthday. His mother's birthday was August.

Theresa: Okay. His mother died before him?

Judy: Yes.

Theresa: Okay. She was the one that met him on the other side. And he hugged his father when he passed. He brought in Saint Michael. Saint Michael is here. So when Saint Michael comes it's either the name Michael; first, middle, last name or nickname. Saint Michael is the patron saint of firefighters and police officers. He's associated with the month of September. Your father-in-law is bringing someone else in. His name could have been Michael. And I'm equal to your father. Why is he pointing upstairs? *Theresa points to the ceiling of the basement she conducted the reading in.* Is that his daughter upstairs?

Judy: Yes.

Theresa: Oh ok. It has to do with her.

Judy: Yeah nothing comes to my mind.

Theresa: Why is is showing me the swan? So let me tell you about the swan. Literally, I go with large swans, but swans mate for life and when their partner dies, that's it. They don't regroup with anybody. For some reason he's saying it's symbolic for someone in the family. Did he mate for life?

Judy: Well my mother-in-law and him were together forever.

Theresa: Now whenever you see a swan now that's your father-in-law saying, 'Call my wife'.

Judy: Well, I'm always with her.

Theresa: If you see one just out of the blue though, call her. Now he is showing me blue. Sky blue. Could be March or December, but he goes more to March. So March could be the third of any month or someone is moving. And let me tell you how I get there. It's because it's Saint Joseph's name day in March and he's the patron Saint of moving and houses.

Judy: Well me and my husband are waiting for my son to get closer to graduation, but we are going to move.

Theresa: No, I don't feel that's why he showed me that particular sign. What's the third? Do you have three children? What's the number three?

Judy: No. We all had two except for me.

Theresa: Okay. I'll let this go for now. But this might be your 'Aha' moment. That means the answer will come to you when you're not actively thinking about it. I'm being shown a breakfront or something that's more vertical than horizontal?

Judy: Do you mean a china cabinet or something like that?

Theresa: Yes. It's taller than it is wider.

Judy: Yeah.

Theresa: What room am I in?

Judy: That's in the dining room.

Theresa: Because this is also where he hangs out.

Judy: That makes sense.

Theresa: Because he still checks to see what's going on. He is telling me there's a water problem here.

Judy: We had a water heater break recently. He was always telling us to make sure we were on top of this stuff. We had to replace it.

Theresa: This is a current event then?

Judy: Yes.

Theresa: Someone's going in for an EKG. I see a monitor of some kind. This is someone who's living. This is not for someone who passed. So either I recently went or I'm going to go for a heart monitor test, or any kind of test where you see the lines. He's going with them. And, actually, I think I'm with his wife. And everything's fine. But someone is going to hurt their wrist. How old is your mother-in-law?

Judy: Seventy-one. A young seventy-one.

Theresa: There's going to be something with her wrists, because she still thinks she's fifty-one. That's what he's saying. She's doing things she shouldn't.

Judy: Yeah. She could already have hurt her wrist. She's always got her hands in the oven.

Theresa: I hear Grace. Do you know a Grace?

Judy: I don't think so.

Theresa: Yes you do, he's saying. What was your gut feeling?

Judy: My mom knows a Grace. But she's not passed.

Theresa: She's not passed. This is someone who's alive. So your mom knows the Grace?

Judy: But it's nobody close to us. I don't know if he would know her.

Theresa: But he does. because he's around. He's telling me it's his current event. It's so funny. He's not letting anyone else in because "I want to talk to you" he's saying. What does he want to tell me about Grace? I don't know if she's feeling too well.

Judy: My mom hasn't spoken to her in a long time. But that's the only Grace I've ever known in my life.

Theresa: Okay. She is going hear something about Grace. He wants that fixed. *points to broken light* That light should not be out, he's saying. I think it might only need a simple twist of the bulb. Who's the left-handed person?

Judy: There's a few. My husband is one.

Theresa: I'm the husband. 1962 or sixty-two. So now I have to do math. Now let's do this. I hate math. The year minus sixty-two but around the age of fifty-three?

Judy: My sister-in-law ▮▮▮ is left handed and she's probably about fifty. We're all very close.

Theresa: Okay. This is his daughter. Is she going to be here today also?

Judy: Yes.

Theresa: So I'm meeting a lot of his girls. You're one of my girls. That's what he's saying. He's sending confirmation. He really loves you.

Judy: I miss him so much.

Theresa: Don't miss him, he's saying. He's around.

Judy: I know he is.

Theresa: Do you have a son?

Judy: Yes.

Theresa: He takes some chances, that one.

Judy: Yes he does. He's actually my father-in-law's namesake.

Theresa: Okay. Now who's ▮▮▮▮▮▮▮▮ or Tony.

Judy: ▮▮▮▮▮▮▮ is his son who is coming here today especially for this.

Theresa: Frank. I'm on the other side. I'm not alive. He's bringing him in.

Judy: I'd have to think. There could be an Uncle Frankie on his side, but I don't know all their family.

Theresa: He's showing me the initials 'FJ' or 'JF'. But this one's alive. Who's the 'FJ' or 'JF'?

Judy: Let's see, he has a son Joseph.

Theresa: Don't think about it too much. He's bringing in a cake. So that means a celebration is coming up. It's not a holiday because they don't show me that. Who's having a birthday or an anniversary? It's not your anniversary.

Judy: Let's see. Who's birthday is coming up? October we're done with birthday's.

Theresa: Then go to November.

Judy: His son Joseph's little boys birthday. My birthday's in November.

Theresa: November what?

Judy: Seventeenth. But I'm trying to think celebration.

Theresa: So he's around with this birthday cake in November. You should celebrate. You don't have to have a party, but you should celebrate. He'll be there.

Judy: Yeah I could see that.

Theresa: Is your husband going to be read?

Judy: No.

Theresa: So this is why he's giving you the messages. His son needs him. So I don't know, for the last three to four months, what's going on near your husband. Whether he thinks about his father more often than not, whether he's angry, whether he's facing something. He makes me feel the last three to four months he's been around him.

Judy: Yeah. He's been really, really busy. And I do think he thinks about his father more than he lets on. We don't even talk about it because I don't want to upset him.

Theresa: Who has the smelly feet? He's making me smell feet. Or who had the body odor towards the end?

Judy: This is from my gut. He had a friend named Johnny. I don't know if it was from his diabetes. We used to joke that they're together.

Theresa: Is that the JF?

Judy: Oh my God! I don't know.

Theresa: He's bringing this gentlemen in. I stink!

Judy: It has to be him. It has to be.

Theresa: He's showing me where he goes. I'm going over a bridge. If I'm your father-in-law I'm going over a bridge. This means he visits someone over a bridge. This breast cancer person is coming in again. This one is definitely on the other side. And I died of it.

Judy: I can't think of anyone close to me.

Theresa: She is definitely here. What are you always straightening up on the wall? Is there a picture that always looks a little crooked?

Judy: I'm always straightening. Everything always looks crooked to me.

Theresa: Okay. Because he shows me you doing that action. He says you do that because of your OCD. Who's Fran? I'm alive not passed. This person is going to need your help.

Judy: Nothing pops out.

Theresa: Okay. Now, he's bringing me near a school. Do you have anything to do with a school?

Judy: Nothing pops out because I'm not really involved.

Theresa: He is mentioning Fran or Francine again. I don't know why. He's telling me that was one of the happiest days of his life, when you married his son. He was beaming. He wants you to start taking pictures. He's going to make himself known in pictures. He's mentioning the month of December or the twelfth of any month. He's hanging onto this December.

Judy: If it's not christmas than I don't know.

Theresa: No they don't show me holidays.

Judy: Unless there's something I don't know about yet.

Theresa: Okay. Do you not go to the cemetery?

Judy: I go to the cemetery.

Theresa: He's grateful to the person who does not go to the cemetery. Is he buried in a cemetery?

Judy: Yes.

Theresa: The reason he's grateful for the person who doesn't go there a lot is because he has to go to the cemetery every time someone goes there to see him. It's annoying to him. So if you could cut down your visits.

Judy: You know what, it's funny because I pass it on the way to work. I don't go in it, but I'm always like "Hey". I can ask my mother-in-law because she doesn't get there as much as she likes.

Theresa: I'm telling you, he's grateful. Which one of his daughters suffers from anxiety. Is that Lisa?

Judy: There's another one, Maria.

Theresa: He's saying it's so unnecessary.

Judy: He told her that in real life too.

Theresa: She's just making it harder and harder. He wants you to get a statue of Saint Michael because that's his patron saint.

Judy: Ok. I'll go get one.

Theresa: And who's ███████ or Dom?

Judy: My father-in-law's brother ███████. He's passed.

Theresa: Dom wants to say hello to you. Something about his shoes. Was he not wearing the right shoes when he was buried? Something about shoes.

Judy: I'd have to ask my mother-in-law, but it's like a joke. He could have on sweatpants or jeans and always have the same shoes. His shoes were his shoes. That it. The same ones. There was like one pair and that was it.

Theresa: Now whose name is Smith? It's either Smitty or Smith or everyone says they were with Smith'?

Judy: My mother-in-law would know.

Theresa: Am I reading her?

Judy: Yeah.

Theresa: I hope he reminds me during her reading. It's so funny. He came in because of your grandmother. Wow! I'm just realizing this. This is your husband's family that came through.

Judy: They're my whole world.

Theresa: So this next girl coming down, she's my April person.

Judy: Yes.

Theresa: She holds in anger, he's saying.

Judy: Maybe.

Theresa: And Millie. Who's Millie?

Judy: That's his other grandmother. His mom, it's her mom. Oh Nan.

Theresa: He puts a queen's tiara on you.

Judy: Oh okay.

Theresa: Because you have the exact opposite personality. But to him, you are the princess in a very loving way. Normally you say "oh she thinks she's a princess".

Judy: Sometimes when I speak of myself I say 'Oh the princess is getting hot.' I bust my own self.

Theresa: Oh so that's why he puts the tiara on you. It's a nickname.

Judy: It's a nickname I gave myself.

Chapter 6

EVERYONE IS GIFTED

As I grew, I continued to grow my gifts. I say "my" gift because everyone's gift is different. And I do mean "everyone" as we are all in possession of psychic abilities. For example, my daughter, also named Theresa, is gifted with sight, though she only saw black and only once. She could make out a body, but it did not come through solid or in color. My son Anthony is able to hear the other side and my son Michael, well the best way I can explain it is to say he's similar to me. He's a warrior that often deals with heavy energy brought by others.

History has documented psychics and mediums since ancient times. It wasn't uncommon to find psychics in royal courts of the past giving advice on anything from crop failure to battles. Nostradamus predicted numerous events and left his legacy in pen and ink artfully written in quatrains - four line predictions. Mediums existed all over the world and were respected members of society. But truth be told, all of us are gifted. Unfortunately, society has taught us that communicating with Spirit is wrong, evil or made up. But that hasn't always been taught as truth. Many ancient belief systems practiced spiritual communications. They nurtured their gifts and learned to fine tune them. They didn't fear them or obey them.

They simply coexisted. Two planes in one existence - energies past and energies present.

Everyone is born gifted. Some of us recognize it very young, like me, and are basically raised alongside it. Some of us won't delve into this part of our makeup until curiosity compels us to do so. We seek answers and go to a psychic, or read a horoscope, or have a premonition that comes true and leaves us seeking even more answers. And the answers will come. And so will more questions. And so is the way of the worlds.

When you first begin using your gifts, spirit will come to you when you're in a dream state. There are two reasons behind this. First and foremost, any spirit that comes from the light wouldn't want to scare you. Getting a visit from your grandmother in a dream seems a lot less frightening than seeing her floating down the hallway. Many would argue that it wouldn't matter either way. They either would or wouldn't want to see her. If they choose not to see her they turn their gifts off and block her out. They will never see her with their primary eyes. Although to me, seeing someone floating down a hallway is normal. Imagine what school must have been like. Half the kids must have been only visible to me. I wonder how many were truly in my graduating class. The second reason spirit will only come when your sleeping is because it's easier for them to get through. When we sleep, our analytical skills are asleep too. Our conscious isn't there to tell us it's wrong to see them or that they no longer exist.

As I mentioned before, there's a big difference between a dream and a visit during dream state. Dreams are fuzzy: the details of them non-sequential and easily forgotten. It involves none of your five primary senses. A visit, however, feels real. The events of seeing and talking to your loved one feels so real you'd swear it actually happened. That's because it did. A visit involves at least one of your primary senses. You can feel their hand, smell their cologne, feel the pressure of their arms around you when they hugged you goodbye.

Some of us subconsciously know that we aren't ready to go past this point. I say subconsciously because on the surface we would all love to see our dearly departed again, but the reality of that visit would scare us. Rather than frighten, Spirit comes through many ways.

Those of us gifted with psychic smell often receive our signs in the form of an old familiar scent. When my sister smells cigarettes, she knows our dad is near. She doesn't want to see him because she knows she would be frightened if she turned to see him standing in the corner, or sitting on the couch. But she can "see" when she's asleep because it's easier for her to accept his presence.

If, as an adult, you wish to progress all the way to sight, it will come in time. Do your research and learn how to protect and discern amongst the spirits. You can't just jump in without learning the rules. When the student is ready, the teacher will come. All you have to do is ask for guidance and the guidance will find you, but it will be on *their* time schedule, not yours.

I can't remember how old I was when I started passing messages between worlds. When I was younger and the world made less sense, I received my signs with my primary senses. I could see things that weren't there with my primary eyes, smell things that weren't around with my primary nose and hear whispers as acute as a breath with my primary ears. Most people would miss it unless you take the time to fine-tune your gift, as I have.

I soon adjusted from using my primary senses to my sixth sense. Now the signs are a bit more subtle. I see images in my mind's eye. It allows me to gather more information much quicker. An image will appear, right out of left field and it'll make no sense to me but all the sense in the world to the person I tell it to. Sometimes stranger's loved ones come to me in dream state prior to them crossing my path and give me a message. I always felt compelled to relay the message. It was a pull that was hard to ignore. Believe me. I tried. Most of the time I gave the message. Sometimes I let my ego impede my gift.

In the mid-eighties, I worked in the office of a security company along with two retired detectives - Rich and Harry.

Rich needed heart surgery. One day he approached my desk and asked if I thought he had a good chance of surviving the operations. I asked him why he wanted my opinion? I honestly wanted to know why considering neither him nor Harry knew about my abilities.

"I don't know", was his reply.

Standing in front of me was a man I knew and respected - a forlorn expression strewn across his entire body. He was desperate. Desperate for hope. Desperate for salvation. Seeking answers. He wasn't seeking my gifts. He needed a friend. So I answered him the best I could, as his friend and not as a medium, although my gut told me this was serious. Very serious.

"You'll be fine."

He had the operation a few days later. That was the last time I saw him alive. I can't say it was the last time I saw him, however. Some months later he interrupted a dream I was having. I don't remember what I was dreaming about before he arrived.

"Please tell my wife I'm going to visit her father soon," he requested. Rich's father-in-law was living. I thought nothing of it when I woke up the next morning and went on with my day like normal.

The following night the same thing happened. Rich once again interrupted my dream. This time he asked me if I delivered his message to his wife yet. I knew this was a dream so didn't feel the need to answer him. I had not reached out to his wife yet. I barely knew the lady and didn't feel like having another one of those awkward "you're going to think I'm crazy" moments.

The next night I walked into my bedroom and immediately sensed a spirit. Standing next to my end table was Rich. He looked me straight in the eye.

"Did you tell my wife about me visiting her father?"

"No. I did not," I replied.

Rich looked disappointed and disappeared. The next morning at work we were notified by Rich's wife that her father had passed away earlier in the day.

I felt awful. Truly awful. I wonder how she would have spent her day if I ignored my ego and delivered that message. I wonder if his wife would have done anything different if she'd known her father's time was close. Would she have been at peace knowing her husband was the one to help him cross? Would I have been able to save her even a little pain? Maybe, but I'll never know because I was too embarrassed to tell her when it counted. I vowed right then and there from now on I would always deliver a message and I would never let my ego get in the way again.

Years past. Now I'm in my forties. I took a brief trip to Arizona to meet a woman that also used to speak to the Virgin Mother. During that trip I found a book with an angel on it that looked like my daughter Theresa. I purchased it and it changed my world. I discovered books about angels, mediums; spirituality on my level. I had never read books written by people like me. I didn't read them for instruction. I read them for clarity. They helped confirm what I already knew was true. I remember asking the Virgin Mother why she stood on a snake and why she had sparkles. I learned what the snake represented years ago. This book, however, mentioned the sparkles and how they were actually angels. Clarity.

My next trip brought me to Aruba - a dream vacation. There I was sitting on the beach reading a book about communicating with spirits; comparing it to my own ways when along comes a lady walking along the beach. I felt her husband wanted to talk to her. I really didn't want to bother her, but felt compelled to do so. I approached with the same line I always started with. It seemed to make getting to the point a lot easier than stumbling through unneeded small talk.

"I know you're going to think I'm crazy, but..."

I delivered messages from her husband who had passed just a few months prior. He wanted her to know that he was proud of her for going into grief counseling. He wanted her to know that she would survive the mourning process and start counseling those grieving. You could see some weight being lifted off her shoulders. She said that she was thinking about becoming a grief counselor, but was on the fence. Her husband needed me to help provide her with the sign she was waiting for. Then she told me something.

She went to a psychic before embarking on her Aruba vacation. She said the psychic had told her she was to meet a woman on a beach that was going to give her a message that would change her life. Turns out that woman was me. I still wonder whatever happened to her.

Chapter 6 ½

MARIA'S READING

Theresa: In that purple box are pencils. Please open it up, choose one using a gut feeling. Rub it. *slight pause* Wow. You got the one. You got it.

Maria: What do I got?

Theresa: You got the right pencil.

Maria: I did?

Theresa: Yup.

Maria: Is that a good thing?

Theresa: That is such a good thing. Rub it. You listened to your gut feeling.

Maria: Serious?

Theresa: I'm not kidding. You should trust your gut more. Give it to me.

Maria puts the pencil back in the tin.

Theresa: You put it back?

Maria: Which one was it? I think it was this one.

Theresa: Redo it. Rub it again. You screwed yourself up. Your father's laughing. He's saying, 'this is her personality. She does this. She second guesses herself. She gets anxiety. And then she has to start all over again. She wastes time.'

Maria: That is so true.

Theresa: You are his psychic daughter. He's telling me to point out to you that he helped you choose the shirt you're wearing.

Maria: Yeah?

Theresa: You thought you chose that shirt. You did not. You want to know why you're wearing that shirt? Because it's your father's favorite color.

Maria: Oh my god!

Theresa: Does that make sense to you?

Maria: Yes!

Theresa: I'm having pain in my leg. Someone around you is having pains in their legs. I don't know if it's your mother. Is it your mom? Does this make sense to you?

Maria: Yes.

Theresa: It's mom.

Maria: Yes.

Theresa: He's concerned about that.

Maria: He should be.

Theresa: Yeah. So should she. He doesn't have dread attached to it. But she tends to think "ah it's nothing, it's nothing", but she's forgetting how it feels to cause worry in his children. He's already given you the answer, 'I'm not that concerned about it', but she should go get it checked for the sake of her children. He's sorry that he caused so much upset and worry about him. He's showing me a soccer ball. Who used to play soccer? Does someone have a little boy who has a ball in the house? That's where I'm going.

Maria: My brother's son plays soccer all the time.

Theresa: There ya go. Okay. That's where he's going. How old is this son?

Maria: Two. He'll be three.

Theresa: Watch what he looks at. Your father talks to that little kid on a daily basis. Now listen, he wants you to stay sober, don't have the drink of wine when you go visit that house. You may see this child playing catch. He'll throw the ball and the ball will come back. He will be playing with your father. You'll only see it once. Don't get nervous. That's just your father playing with his grandson.

Maria: Oh my god.

Theresa: You need signs like that.

Maria: Right.

Theresa: He puts creativity near you. There's a uniqueness here. Everyone else came out of the same egg, but not you.

Maria: Yes. I've always heard that.

Theresa: Dad is giving you the moon. He's saying, because it's more the moon, for you, that gives you power over the sun. It's not even the full moon. You don't need the full moon. You just need a little tiny piece of the moon.

Maria: Yup.

Theresa: And you're more comfortable and, for you, clarity comes at night.

Maria: Yes.

Theresa: Who has the cat?

Maria: Nobody anymore.

Theresa: Who had that cat?

Maria: He did. My mom and him.

Theresa: This cat is meowing, meowing, meowing, meowing right now.

Maria: He's with the cat now?

Theresa: The cat is with him.

Maria: Oh.

Theresa: He's showing me a bobcat. Not the cat bobcat. He wants me to tell you your uncle Bob is here. And your Uncle ████████'s here.

Maria: Did he tell you those names?

Theresa: Yes. Your father's telling me to 'introduce everybody, please, to my daughter.' There might be a reason he's telling me this. So use your gut feeling, not your brains. Okay? He's showing me a bobcat which is a construction type of thing. Who's thinking about doing construction in the house? Who's digging a hole? It's construction. Now it could be a thought, or it could actually be going on.

Maria: I'd have to think about that.

Theresa: Dad is pointing to your stomach area. The energy is off in your stomach. Do you suffer with stomach pains? Did you have a miscarriage or anything? *Theresa gestures to her own stomach.* All of this area is hurting me. So I could get an anxious stomach; a nervous stomach.

Maria: Yeah. I'm his nervous child.

Theresa: Oh. You are.

Maria: Nothing wrong though, right?

Theresa: No. You do it to yourself. Most of his daughters do it to themselves.

Maria: Yeah.

Theresa: Part of your problem - because he's a doctor now...

Maria: He's always been a doctor.

Theresa: So here's his diagnosis for you. He's telling me to tell you, you have a little mental OCD. For example, let's say you see an acorn, and you're ready to pick it up. You have to get it out of the way, then you think, wait a minute, there has to be a reason this acorn is here. What if it's a squirrel gathering these acorns because she knows the winter is coming? Now if I move this acorn, she's never going to find it. That means she could be starving to death, etcetera. Does that make sense to you?

Maria: That makes perfect sense.

Theresa: That's your OCD diagnosis, he's saying. You're welcome. He's funny.

Maria: Oh he's funny. You have no idea. I know he's watching over me.

Theresa: All of you.

Maria: I know that. I know that.

Theresa: All of you.

Maria: We just don't know how to feel it, or understand the coincidences they try to communicate through.

Theresa: It's through coincidence and it's through your gut feeling. That's how dad talks to you. Especially about this little boy.

Maria: I wonder why that one, and not the other, he's talking about.

Theresa: I don't know. He's mentioning, Nick or Nicholas?

Maria: My nephew.

Theresa: Is this the same one we were just talking about?

Maria: No. My other one.

Theresa: He's talking about Nicholas.

Maria: What about it?

Theresa: He could be swayed by other people. So go with your gut feeling when dealing with him. Nick. Or Nicholas.

Maria: It's funny you say both the names because he goes by both. Nick to us and Nicholas to his parents.

Theresa: Do you believe in reincarnation? Your father is attaching you to the twenties. The nineteen twenties.

Maria: Really?

Theresa: So what is it with you and the nineteen twenties? Do you like jazz? Do you like fashion from there? There's something with the nineteen twenties for you.

Maria: People were just so much nicer back then.

Theresa: So you were dropped here. I mean you came here the regular way, but you had to come right back. You were in the twenties.

Maria: Really?

Theresa: Yes. I have no doubt about that. That's what he's telling me. Do you like dancing?

Maria: Yes! I love dancing.

Theresa: There you go. You were a flapper. You used to sing also.

Maria: I did? I love singing. I think I'm good but I'm not.

Theresa: You're carrying it over from another lifetime.

Maria: I used to dance and sing in the twenties?

Theresa: Yes. You're a twenties girl, but you had to come right back. I don't think you killed yourself, but you died very young, but through your own actions. Meaning, I either drank too much or something happened. You were with a partner. And you could have been easily influenced. You were influenced by others to try to fit in. This time around you don't care if you fit in. I feel like, 'I don't fit in. Nobody gets me'. This time around you put a positive spin on being unique. You don't care about fitting in. It's now the same thing with this nephew that he told you to go with your gut feeling. He could be easily swayed because he wants to fit in. That's why you can help him out.

Maria: And I'm such a goodie today.

Theresa: There is going to be a Sam in your life, your father is saying.

Maria: A Sam?

Theresa: Yeah. Who's Sam or Samuel? Could be first, middle, last name or nickname. Or something Sam's. You will benefit from a Sam.

Maria: I don't know.

Theresa: Who is Lorraine?

Maria: Lorraine?

Theresa: Yes. go with your gut feeling. Don't think about.

Maria: First person that comes to mind is my husband's side. Cousin. Third? Second?

Theresa: There's a story that's going to be coming out about Lorraine. Your father is a gossiper, just so you know.

Maria: He's a fun guy.

Theresa: It's a funny story about Lorraine. It's going to make sense to you, he's saying.

Maria: I don't even think he knew her.

Theresa: Even better.

Maria: Really?

Theresa: Because he knows her now. What does that prove to you? Life goes on.

Maria: Wow.

Theresa: Even for him, life goes on.

Maria: Wow.

Theresa: Now, this little two year old grandson, was he born after your father's passing?

Maria: Yes.

Theresa: Alright. He's playing with him so of course he knows Lorraine. You have to start connecting the dots, he's saying to you. Connect the dots.

Maria: Gosh, it makes sense.

Theresa: Yeah, most of the time I trust them enough where I will be led by them because they'll help me get an acknowledgment for their signs. He's showing me a tunnel. 'This is not the tunnel that you pass through upon death,' your father's saying. I'm actually driving through a tunnel. Who used to go through the tunnel?

Maria: Well, when we were little he took us to Virginia Beach. He had to go through the tunnels.

Theresa: Okay. A memory. Now your father wants to go to the number eight. So it's either August, the eighth of any month or the number eight.

Maria: August eighth?

Theresa: It doesn't have to be. It could be August, the eighth of any month or the number eight. And it's not your grandmother's passing because I think your grandmother passed in August.

Maria: That's what I'm thinking of.

Theresa: They're already saying it's not that.

Maria: Let's see. I'm not really good with numbers that much.

Theresa: Okay. Just keep that in mind. I'm going to circle the eight. Do you know a Stacey yet?

Maria: I know a Stacey.

Theresa: He's talking about a Stacey.

Maria: I know a few.

Theresa: When was the last time you spoke about or to any of these Stacey's?

Maria: I don't frequently see them. In conversations, I might have spoken with friends about them, maybe. I don't know. A couple of months ago, maybe.

Theresa: Okay. Is this a friend of yours?

Maria: No. My sister-in-law's friend. She's not really a close friend. But then there's another Stacey on another side and we talk about her as well.

Theresa: Stacey's kind of into these things. This is a Stacey that believes in this stuff.

Maria: I'm trying to think which one it could be. I only know two.

Theresa: There's going to be a reconnection with a Stacey who's into this stuff.

Maria: Alright. That makes sense then.

Theresa: I feel as if I have swollen feet. Did someone have diabetes, sugar problem, or had swollen feet?

Maria: That passed?

Theresa: One passed. One is here. So let's go with the one that passed. I didn't have to die from it, but I had it. I either had sugar problems...

Maria: My grandmother kind of had sugar.

Theresa: Is this the grandmother associated with the number eight?

Maria: Yeah.

Theresa: There's someone here, living, who also has this problem.

Maria: Her daughter, yeah.

Theresa: Your father's saying 'watch with the one...'

Maria: She's diabetic.

Theresa: Okay. Dad wants me to mention Mondays. Was anybody born on a Monday, passed on a Monday? Something with Monday. Did dad do something special on Mondays?

Maria: For him every day was special.

Theresa: I would love to live like him.

Maria: Every day was his day. Um, Monday? Every day runs into every day for me.

Theresa: No, he's being pretty specific.

Maria: Monday? Monday?

Theresa: Does someone in your family, your immediate family do something on Mondays?

Maria: Just the regular school stuff.

Theresa: No.

Maria: Monday. No sports are on Mondays. Oh!

Theresa: Go ahead...

Maria: The card game Monday nights. Not me. But yes, there are card games Monday nights.

Theresa: Okay. There you go. So your father is confirming that he's there.

Maria: That's so funny.

Theresa: Someone cheats.

Maria: Oh yeah.

Theresa: You know that?

Maria: Oh yeah. We know who it is too.

Theresa: Dad throws everybody under the bus. And then he laughs about it. 'You didn't hear that from me.' He's showing me a charm. It may have a picture. Do you know what he's trying to show me?

Maria: A charm with a picture?

Theresa: He's showing me.

Maria: A little heart shape.

Theresa: Yeah, but it looks like an image of someone on it.

Maria: We did give my mother a heart shaped charm with a picture. But it's a bracelet.

Theresa: That's ok. But it has to have the charm on it.

Maria: Yeah. So he sees that?

Theresa: He loves that. He puts the color red near you though. So that's either January or July. Why is he putting the red near you?

Maria: January or July? My son was born in July.

Theresa: There you go. That's why. That's how easy this is.

Maria: It's so simple. You see me thinking.

Theresa: Now your father is saying, don't think. They speak to us through coincidences. You went for the right pencil, okay. But then you dropped it, whatever, and then you had to think and then pick it up.

Maria: You know I did that with my shirt. I had a different color shirt than I put this on right before I left.

Theresa: There you go. Because now you got the right color shirt on. It's his color.

Maria: And I thought I did this on my own. I'm thinking I didn't like the beige. I liked the blue.

Theresa: That's how subtle the signs they give us can be. And it's always by coincidence and not thought.

Maria: I think too much.

Theresa: Too much. Because your father's saying you can analyze a piece of shit.

Maria: Tell him thank you. That's exactly right.

Theresa: And you create such frustration within yourself. And then you chastise yourself. And then you get the anxiety and you're in a cycle.

Maria: Oh my God! You're right! Ask him how I undo all this.

Theresa: Eliminate the brain. Get rid of the need to always be right and not make a mistake. That's a big difference, for my daughter, he's saying.

Maria: Yes. Oh, my God.

Theresa: So now, he puts red near you again.

Maria: July's my son's birthday.

Theresa: So he's reaching out to your son. That son was supposed to be yours. He's an old soul, that son.

Maria: Yes.

Theresa: You will learn from that son. Eventually, the roles will be reversed. He's a very old soul. He'll help you with this.

Maria: Yeah.

Theresa: He puts the initial "P" near you. Do you know a Paul?

Maria: Yes.

Theresa: Who's Paul?

Maria: He's an old friend. Like years back. But there's a Paul that lives right next to my mother. Always watches out for her.

Theresa: That's who it is. Because dad is sending gratitude to Paul. You have to play more music in the house. There used to be more music, he's saying.

Maria: Yeah.

Theresa: He's talking about evergreen plants. It's the evergreens. Did anyone recently plant evergreens?

Maria: Yes!

Theresa: Why?

Maria: We planted a tree for him.

Theresa: It's the evergreen?

Maria: Yes. It comes to flowers, but it was green when we planted it.

Theresa: Okay. Where is it?

Maria: It's in the back of my mother's house.

Theresa: Can you plant around that?

Maria: It's a garden.

Theresa: He's talking about the evergreens in that area. Are there evergreens in that area where in the winter you'll still see green?

Maria: Yeah. There's green there.

Theresa: Good. Because that's his focal point. Who's really into makeup?

Maria: I love makeup.

Theresa: Do you experiment with it?

Maria: That's my daughter. And my sister likes makeup. The three of us.

Theresa: Dad is referring to your daughter. How old is she?

Maria: Sixteen.

Theresa: Did she start driving yet?

Maria: She started just thinking about her permit. We don't want to. She's not ready.

Theresa: And don't force her, your father's saying.

Maria: No.

Theresa: Dad put the color purple around you. Purple is the color for February.

Maria: My mother's birthday.

Theresa: Believe it or not, your mother pays more attention to what you say than you think she does.

Maria: Really?

Theresa: That's what your father is saying.

Maria: Is he content? Is he happy? I know he misses us.

Theresa: He does. He feels bad for not being here, but he is near his family in another form. You won't see him, but you can feel him when you aren't over thinking any signs he's trying to send to you. He's not going to do the butterfly thing, but with you, he is going to be leaving silver coins because you could use the money, he's saying. So if you find the nickels, dimes and quarters - he doesn't leave pennies for you - pick them up and save them. He doesn't like masks near you. Do you celebrate Halloween?

Maria: No.

Theresa: Good. Okay. That's why. You're not really Halloween person.

Maria: I used to go with the kids, but now they're too old.

Theresa: He's telling me… he's waiting to speak to mom. Is she waiting for a reading?

Maria: Yes.

Chapter 7

SNOW ON THE BEACH

My mother never seemed to put two-and-two together about my gifts - even after the Aunt Tessie incident. Plus, there was another time that should have clued her in. I was eight.

After giving me three sisters, Mom had a set of twins - boy and girl. Since I was her oldest, I was assigned to help with one and they assigned my second oldest sister to the other. I got the girl.

My baby sister came down with an awful ear infection, so bad my mom had to bring her to the hospital. My Aunt Irene (still living at the time) had a bad feeling about it. She said, "Get her out of the hospital or they'll kill her. Bring her home and she'll be alright." Mom listened, signed her out and brought her home.

That night I stood in the living room. From there I could see into Mom's bedroom where my baby sister lay in her crib. Next to her crib stood the Virgin Mother and Saint Joseph.

Mom saw me and called me into her room where she had been sitting on her bed. She said she'd seen the Virgin Mother and Saint Joseph come towards the crib and she knew my little sister would be alright. She asked if I had seen them too. I told her yes. That was the last time we ever spoke together about Spirit until almost half a century later. And boy what a half century it's been.

I spent my life looking for my "soul" mate. I pictured him tall and handsome. He would have a strong belief in God. He would be good to his mother. I was taught to look at how a man treats his mother since that's what I'd be in store for when the novelty of being a newlywed wore off.

Being brought up in an Italian household, my father had given me two possible choices of moving out. The first was to be married, the second was to be carried out in a coffin. Hence, the reason for my first marriage which resulted in two beautiful sons. My second marriage was to my high school sweetheart. We produced a beautiful daughter and after eleven years of marriage went our separate ways. Since I was the good daughter when I was young, I never went to a bar, or to a disco, or hung out with friends. So when the opportunity presented itself to explore the world as an unattached woman, I jumped at the chance and fell flat on my face. I got married again. When that marriage began to fail I decided to enlist the help of a dictionary to see if I'd been thinking about my "soul" mate the wrong way this entire time.

Soul mates: soul mate.[ˈsōl ˌmāt]NOUN .a person ideally suited to another as a close friend or romantic partner.

(Oxford University Press • Translation by Bing 2016)

Definition of soul mate
1: a person who is perfectly suited to another in temperament
2: a person who strongly resembles another in

attitudes or beliefs <ideological soul mates>
soulmate is a relationship that exists on a deeper,
more spiritual level than most of our other
relationships.

My dictionary search didn't produce any profound
insight. As a matter of fact, it left me even more
perplexed as to what I was doing wrong. So I enlisted
the help of my Angels. I wasn't actively searching for
anyone, but I needed to know what and how the term
"soul mate" applied to me. So I made a deal with my
Angels. I love the beach. I'd always wanted to see the
beach covered in snow. Whoever was to be my
soulmate would walk on the beach in the snow with
me.

Twelve years passed and the thought left my mind.
I was divorcing my third husband, but he still lived
with me in my home. It was this point in my life when
Dad needed a helping hand and moved into the room
across the hall from me.

My father was totally against the whole mystic
lifestyle. Once I saw him flipping through the
television channels. Nothing seemed to pique his
interest until he came across a show hosted by a
celebrity psychic. He was immediately hot under the
collar.

"Do you believe this guy? I can't believe people
believe in this! If this was true, I'd have been able to
talk to my sister Tessie after she died."

My gut told me this wasn't the time to come out to
my father. He didn't need to know that not only could I
communicate with the dead, but Aunt Tessie was the
one that taught me how to do it.

Even though I had a secret to keep, I loved having
my father live with me. I was so grateful that I could
provide him with the same amenities he provided for

me when I was young. A roof over his head, food in his belly, warm bed in the winter and clothes on his back. I doted on him.

I returned home from work one day to find my dad watching a baseball game. He looked perplexed. I asked him why he looked confused and he said he was waiting for Babe Ruth to come out of the dugout. Jokingly, I asked him if he was stroking, but he looked so serious that I quickly came to the realization that this was "real" for him. I sat down in the living room and waited for the Babe to come onto the field. After a bit, my dad came to the conclusion that he might have been on the injured list. This was to be the only odd behavior that my father exhibited during his time with me. Needless to say, I kept a close eye on him after that.

We spent a lot of time together. Some days we'd visit relatives. Some days we watched television or sat around talking about anything and everything. Those were the moments I cherished the most.

Dad started sleeping more. First, it was until the afternoon. Then the entire day. Then two days in a row. I constantly went into his room to check on him and make sure everything was okay. One night, after I'd already retired for the evening, I heard a noise in my kitchen. I ran in there to investigate and there was Dad, sitting at the table ready for his morning coffee. I served him a cup, looked him straight in the eye and asked, "Are you feeling ill?"

"I feel fine," he replied.

"Okay," I said. "But promise me you'll let me know if you aren't feeling well so I can bring you to the doctor."

"I promise," he replied, "but you don't have to worry." I watched him sip his coffee and knew he was wrong.

Soon after that morning, I received a phone call from one of my sisters asking if I'd like to go to Atlantic City with her the following Saturday. She prepaid for the room, but wasn't speaking with her boyfriend and didn't want to lose her money. I checked with my husband, since we were still living together at the time, and he confirmed he was planning on staying home for the weekend. He would watch my dad while I went. I let Dad know I was leaving Saturday morning but would be back Sunday afternoon.

My sister and I arrived in Atlantic City early Saturday afternoon. We settled in and unpacked before hitting the boardwalk. Atlantic City is a gambler's paradise. Besides the countless rows of casinos, the boardwalk was full of shops, storefronts, kiosks and street vendors. There was so much to see and do on this crisp sunny day. What did we decide on? A psychic reading. I know what you're thinking. Why would I, of all people, seek psychic advice? I truly go to readers for entertainment purposes. Also, believe it or not, I can't read myself. Besides that I like to see if they can pick up the energy that I have spiritual abilities too.

We found a storefront advertising the psychic inside and went in. As soon as I sat down, the reader asked if my dad was living with me. I confirmed that he was. She then asked if I thought his health was good. I told her I was keeping my eye on him. My dad was in his seventies so this question didn't stir up any concern because it would make sense that an elderly parent would have health issues. I told her that I believed I had a year left with my dad.

My sister sat down and began her reading. It was more of the usual nature I find most readings are like. She was told she'd be making more money soon, things like that. Then she was told that she'd meet the love of her life as the person she was currently with was not her soulmate. I'd heard there was a snowstorm brewing and said aloud that it would be nice to see snow on a beach. The reader laughed at me and said snow never sticks to the sand in Atlantic City because the salt in the air from the water melts it before it lands. She said in all the years she'd been there it's never happened, even during blizzards. We finished our readings, paid the nice lady and left.

We did a little shopping, a little gambling and went to a late dinner at a little restaurant right along the beachfront. We finished our meal around eleven and left the restaurant ready to head back to the hotel. We took one foot outside when I noticed. Not only was it snowing, but the entire beach was covered in fluffy white stuff. I just started laughing. My sister looked at me like I was nuts. I told her that it would be my luck that a sister of mine would be the soul mate I'd been looking for. Then I explained to her my theory of soul mates and the deal I made with my Angels all those years ago. We both had a giggle then made our way back to the hotel to relax and unwind.

When it came time to settle in I went to turn the television off. Before I had a chance to reach the remote, the television turned itself off.

"Must be a spirit in the room," I joked.

I turned the television back on like I'd normally do as I maintain control over any spirit that comes my way. I told my sister I wanted to call Dad and make sure he was alright. She reassured me that my husband was there and it was late. If we tried to call and they didn't answer, we'd only worry until morning and that was no good for either of us. Besides, we were leaving in the morning. So we went to bed, woke up, packed up and drove home.

We lived a few hours from Atlantic City so it took a while to get back. When we were about ten minutes away, my daughter called hysterical. She'd come home from college for a break and noticed the house had an intensely foul odor. She found my dad unconscious in his bed. And where was my soon to by ex-husband? He decided to go to a casino of his own last night. Said he got jealous I got to go, so he went and left Dad alone.

The smell of death met us at the door. I knew what was about to happen. And I reacted the only way I could think of. I had to pee. It was a long car ride and I needed to pee and I just wanted to do that one simple act one more time before my life changed forever. I popped into the bathroom, finished up, washed up, and opened the door to a whole new world. Things would never be the same again.

Dad was a simple man. He had his routines and stuck to them, one of which was his weekly shower ritual. This happened once a week at eleven, right after his show. He must have gone back out to his favorite chair after his shower and got sick. I found the evidence splattered on his cushion. Somehow he made it back to bed, laid down and had a heart attack.

Dad was taken to the emergency room. He would never regain consciousness. He suffered a stroke and was bleeding into his brain. I signed a Do Not Resuscitate Order. He officially passed Monday, January 31st at seven in the evening.

I had often asked my father what January 31st was. He had told me it was nothing. I insisted it was something, but couldn't tell him how I knew it was an important date. I couldn't tell him Spirit put that image in my mind and wouldn't release me of it. He insisted there was nothing special about January 31st and got angry when I wouldn't let it go. After he passed, his sister later revealed to me that January 31st was also the anniversary of my grandfather's passing. - my father's father. He also passed of a sudden heart attack. This was no coincidence.

Like dream state, sometimes our souls travel. In my father's case his soul must have started its journey home when he first had his heart attack and first slipped into his coma around eleven in the evening that Saturday. The exact moment I saw snow on the beach. He was with me right then. He sent the snow. He turned off the television. I now knew he was my soulmate because for the first time I found my meaning of the word soulmate. It had the simplest meaning. While the other definitions also apply soul mates are just that - members of our Soul group from the Other Side. The group we leave when we come here to Earth. The group that looks out for us. Keeps us safe. Loves us unconditionally. Dad always told me no one would ever take care of me as good as he does. And he's right. He was and will always be my one true Soul Mate.

Dad used to sleep in the room directly across the hall from my bedroom. Every night I heard the clickety-clack of tiny nails marching across the wood floor. My two dogs followed Dad wherever he went - along with my three cats. When he sat down in his maroon recliner to watch the news at night, the two dogs and three cats all somehow managed to squeeze in that chair with him. When he went to bed, all six of them - Dad included - somehow fit on his twin sized bed. After Dad passed the dogs wouldn't set foot in his room even though it remained unchanged. Instead, they chose to sleep on my bedroom floor.

It took Dad a few months before he started leaving

signs to let us know he was around. First, he appeared to my daughter in a very subtle manner, so he wouldn't cause fear. She called me into her room one night and told me to look at her television. It was off. Completely off. On the screen was an image of my dad's profile. Sometimes signs are so subtle that you'd miss them if you didn't pay attention. His personal lounge chair would start to smell like him, but only if I was upset. Dad was around. I could feel him, but nothing more than that.

I went on with life the way one needs to. I woke up and went to work every day. Then I'd come home, take care of my family and, most often, read myself to sleep at night only to wake and repeat the next morning. I thought it was just another night. I finished chapter nine of my book and put it on the nightstand. I shut off the light, turned onto my right side, and started my evening prayers. I'd decided long ago that praying is praying whether you're on your knees or not. Besides, I was at the age where if I got on my knees to pray the entire prayer would be that I could get back up. I finished with an "Amen" still facing the wall. Behind me, I could hear the dogs wagging their tails against the wooden floor. They began to swish back and forth faster and faster.

At this point in my life, I was living alone again, so I slept with Dad's butcher knife by my side. I grabbed the knife and flipped on the light ready to fend for myself. Right in front of my eyes - and in front of the dogs - stood my father. He had a look of disbelief on his face like he couldn't believe I could see him. I didn't want him to be confused or mad at me for seeing him so I just smiled, turned the light off and went to sleep. After that night, my dogs would go in and out of his bedroom throughout the day and occasionally slept there at night.

Chapter 7 ½

ANTOINE'S READING

Theresa: Your father wanted to pass alone, but who was there?

Antoine: Who was there?

Theresa: Were you all there?

Antoine: Yeah. We were all there at some point.

Theresa: He wanted to pass alone 'because I wanted to save them from this'. My whole throat is hurting me now. Keep in mind that I'm intuitive so anything I feel does not belong to me. It's a way they communicate signs to me. First, we'll go with; why is my whole throat hurting me? Did he have a tube down the throat? Was there something with his throat? What's with the throat?

Antoine: Coughing?

Theresa: It's sore.

Antoine: Emphysema.

Theresa: Okay. But did your father ever have a tube down his throat for a test? Or something with a tube down his throat?

Antoine: Yes.

Theresa: He hated that. Hated it.

Antoine: He did.

Theresa: I was ready to put my own bullet in my head, he says. Dad's showing me a big ring. Who has this ring now? It almost looks like a nugget ring.

Antoine: I don't know.

Theresa: Who suffers with the nerves or anxiousness?

Antoine: The two most nervous, anxious people would be my two sisters.

Theresa: Who's Tony?

Antoine: I'm Tony.

Theresa: Oh, you're Tony. So are you known as both? Antoine and Tony?

Antoine: Yeah. Antoine to the family and Tony to outside.

Theresa: That's so funny. I'm Theresa to family and Terry to outside. Who's around fifty years old?

Antoine: I'm fifty three.

Theresa: What event happened in nineteen-sixty-six that changed the matrix of the family?

Antoine: I was four. I don't know.

Theresa: Did anybody pass in your father's family when you were around four years old?

Antoine: Not that I know of.

Theresa: He's making me feel there was a big change in the family makeup when you were around four years old. I feel there's a loss. He wants to introduce you to everybody that's here because he's holding court today. Your uncle ███████████.

Antoine: Yup.

Theresa: Your uncle ███████████.

Antoine: Yup.

Theresa: Your grandmother ███████████.

Antoine: Yup.

Theresa: Who's Frank?

Antoine: I don't know.

Theresa: He circles the number six. It's either June, the sixth of any month of the number six means something to somebody.

Antoine: The only thing that jumps at me is six was my first football number.

Theresa: There ya go. So it's the number six. He said your football games were important to him. He's telling me you used to put fingerprints all over the place.

Antoine: Uh huh.

Theresa: Does that make sense to you?

Antoine: Yeah! Yeah, it does.

Theresa: He's telling me, "this kid always had his hands on everything."

Antoine: I think that still goes on.

Theresa: Do you? You still do it?

Antoine: Yeah.

Theresa: Who's ███████████?

Antoine: He's my brother. Second youngest brother.

Theresa: He's not here.

Antoine: Not yet. He's coming soon for his reading.

Theresa: Dad wants to make sure you know that he doesn't want your mother to do anything.

Antoine: Yup.

Theresa: She shouldn't have to shovel the snow off her car. Nothing. He worries. Does she live alone?

Antoine: Yes.

Theresa: She's in good health, but she keeps too much in. He's saying your mother doesn't let onto what's really going on. That's what I used to do. Then everyone gets mad at you because everyone's saying if we knew this we probably would or wouldn't have...

Antoine: Oh, right.

Theresa: He's switching topics. Who used to go clamming? He's showing me clams.

Antoine: The only thing with clams that comes to memory is my first vacation.

Theresa: Where's that?

Antoine: Virginia Beach.

Theresa: Were you the one that was golfing recently?

Antoine: No.

Theresa: One of the brothers? Somebody was golfing. Or a brother-in-law was golfing.

Antoine: Yup.

Theresa: You need to learn to relax a little, he's saying.

Antoine: Oh yes.

Theresa: You don't.

Antoine: No.

Theresa: You're killing yourself with stress.

Antoine: That's one-hundred percent correct.

Theresa: You also have a tendency of keeping things in.

Antoine: Yes.

Theresa: You feel as if you don't want to worry anybody. Or you just don't want to talk about it. Or even better, if I don't acknowledge it, it doesn't exist - just like your dad and mom do.

Antoine: Yeah. Yup.

Theresa: Dad is showing me someone punching a wall.

Antoine: Yeah.

Theresa: He's showing me a seafood restaurant. He's worried about someone eating the seafood. So either someone eats the raw sushi or the raw clams and he's worried about that. Dad points to mom. Raw clams. Not so much sushi. Clams. He says to tell her not to eat too many raw clams. It can bother her kidneys.

Antoine: Yeah.

Theresa: Dad's telling me you're not a complicated person.

Antoine: No.

Theresa: It is what it is.

Antoine: Yup.

Theresa: That sometimes is a positive thing and sometimes it's a negative thing.

Antoine: Absolutely.

Theresa: Because I get a sad heart, because of the way I am.

Antoine: Yes.

Theresa: Does that make sense to you?

Antoine: Yeah. Yeah.

Theresa: Dad is telling me a doorknob has to be replaced or someone is having problems with keys fitting in a lock. He tells me it's in Mom's house. He has a punch list for you to do for Mom by the way - just so you know.

Antoine: I'm sure.

Yeah. He's very concerned about your mother.

Antoine: He always was.

Theresa: Very concerned. He's mentioning ██████.

Antoine: ▮▮▮▮▮ is my brother Joe's, wife's, first child from another marriage.

Theresa: How old is he?

Antoine: He just graduated high school and I think he's on his way to the service.

Theresa: Very good. Dad will visit him while ▮▮▮▮▮ is over there. He puts a question mark near ▮▮▮▮. In other words, it could go one way or the other, but he's not showing me anything bad.

Antoine: Right.

Theresa: He makes me feel that it's good he's going in the service.

Antoine: I think we all agree. It's probably a good thing.

Theresa: Dad thinks it's a good idea too. It was necessary for him to enlist and it's also necessary for his mother - or your brother's family - because they need the distance and they need the rest.

Antoine: Yup.

Theresa: 'They do need the rest', your fathers saying.

Antoine: I got it.

Theresa: Who has the black and white wedding photo out?

Antoine: The black and white wedding photo out?

Theresa: Now it could be one of your sisters, you, your mother. But it's black and white.

Antoine: Not sure. Probably would be one of my sisters I guess.

Theresa: When you see that picture, or the photo album out, that is the sister that listens to what's not being said so she can help you with mom.

Antoine: True. Yes.

Theresa: Who thought they had a hernia or appendix or pain in the...?

Antoine: Gallbladder. I had.

Theresa: Okay. Dad makes me feel you thought it was going to something else. He is now mentioning twins.

Antoine: The only twins I come across...

Theresa: Gut feeling. Go with it.

Antoine: ... are my wife's nephews.

Theresa: He puts problems on that side of the family.

Antoine: Yup. Some.

Theresa: Okay. Because he keeps going to that side of the family. That's a source of problems and it trickles into your house.

Antoine: Sometimes it does, yeah.

Theresa: Now you don't need to borrow problems. You got your own stuff, your father's saying. He's showing me a firehouse. Is anyone a fireman? Or a volunteer? Why is he showing me a firehouse? Or did somebody live near a firehouse?

Antoine: Our old house. The firehouse was up the road.

Theresa: So he's showing me a memory. Remember, he has to keep giving me confirmations throughout this reading. He put the number eleven near you. This can mean the month of November, the eleventh of any month or the number eleven.

Antoine: That makes sense.

Theresa: It's not your father's birthday, he's saying.

Antoine: I know.

Theresa: What's the eleven near you?

Antoine: That would be my son's month.

Theresa: And how old is he?

Antoine: Twenty-one.

Theresa: Now, not you, but there is an initial 'A' near him.

Antoine: Yes.

Theresa: Why?

Antoine: His first name is Antoine.

Theresa: So he's a junior of yours?

Antoine: He's Antoine ███████████.

Theresa: He tells me this son of yours has his head on straight - even for a twenty-one-year-old. So not for you to ride him, so much. Or worry about him so much.

Antoine: Yeah he does.

Theresa: I told you your grandmother is here, right?

Antoine: Yes.

Theresa: She's stepping forward. She just wanted to be acknowledged. She'll wait to see if Dad ever stops talking. Dad said it's time for a weekend. You need to go fishing, he's saying.

Antoine: Yeah.

Theresa: You have to because you're burning out. And you know it, but you're not doing anything about it. You're stubborn. You might as well have been the Taurus. Who is the Taurus in the family?

Antoine: The stubborn one?

Theresa: Yeah.

Antoine: That would be my brother ██████████.

Theresa: Okay.

Antoine: Yeah.

Theresa: Dad puts the initial "M" near you. Do you know a Mitch? Or the initial "M"?

Antoine: Um.

Theresa: Does your son have a friend named Mitch?

Antoine: Yes.

Theresa: That's where I'm going.

Antoine: Yes.

Theresa: Is he going out with Mitch this Halloween?

Antoine: Probably.

Theresa: Your father doesn't like the energy near your son.

Antoine: I don't either.

Theresa: Okay. 'So do something about it', your father is saying. I don't know what you can do when they're twenty-one.

Antoine: Yeah.

Theresa: Dad doesn't like this Mitch character.

Antoine: Wow.

Theresa: He shows me a sailboat. Did anybody make a sailboat when they were younger? And Dad is mentioning Montauk, New York.

Antoine: Not a sailboat.

Theresa: What was it then?

Antoine: The only two boats that trigger any kind of info for me...

Theresa: Go ahead.

Antoine: ...it was when we were younger we went to my Uncle Frankie's boat in Long Island, Montauk.

Theresa: There you go!

Antoine: We were on that boat with my cousins and my Uncle Frank.

Theresa: Dad tried to get us to acknowledge Frank earlier in the reading. He was able to do it now through the memory of the boat. He tells me to say the name ███████. Why?

Antoine: They lived right next door.

Theresa: Dad shows me a Plymouth.

Antoine: It was my first car.

Theresa: Dad is showing me St. John's hospital. Who was John?

Antoine: My father's best friend. He is deceased also. That's also the hospital we all went to when we were sick and where John used to work.

Theresa: Okay. So John wants to come in and dad is letting him do so.

Antoine: Really?

Theresa: What's the connection with Yonkers?

Antoine: We were all born and raised in Yonkers.

Theresa: Oh. Not a coincidence. You see how this works? Your father is now trying to help you lift up your shoulders. He's trying to help you with this. But there's a lot. There's a lot.

Antoine: There is a lot going on.

Theresa: Um, he sends a lot of love. But more than the love, he says, is the respect. That, to him, is very important. He respects you because I think he demanded respect. And you respect your father.

Antoine: Oh yes.

Theresa: 'You didn't have to love me', Dad says, 'but you had to respect me.' Now it's his turn to respect his son.

Antoine: Thank you. I appreciate this.

Chapter 8

BENITA GETS A VISITOR

One Monday morning I sat in my office trying to get a grasp on what needed to be done. Nita stormed up to my doorway and stopped there. She had her arms crossed and eyes on the floor.

"I need to talk to you."

Nita was either sick or worried sick because she was white as a ghost - an interesting feat considering she's Puerto Rican. Her skin is usually a beautiful golden brown. She said she needed to tell me a story. She made me promise not to repeat it to anyone in her family.

"You sure you don't want to sit down?" I asked, gesturing to the chair across from my desk.

Again she declined, claiming if she sat her nerves would get the better of her. She still wasn't making eye contact. She just stared off to the side and began to explain.

See, Nita lives with her ailing mother. She's devoted her life to her mother's care. It's just the two of them in their apartment. She told me, for some reason she woke up at 2:28 this morning. Her throat felt dry so she got out of bed and went to the kitchen for a glass of water. She flicked on the light and was shocked to see an old man sitting at her table. She said she screamed and begged the man to spare her mother and herself. She shouted they had no money and lunged for the phone to call the police.

The elderly man spoke up and told her he wasn't there to harm her. He said he wanted to talk to her. He said she could call the police after he was done speaking to her if she still wanted to. He reminded her he was old. What harm could he really do anyway?

She sat down, trembling. She started having thoughts of him not being real so she pinched herself to make sure she wasn't sleeping. The old man looked her straight in the eyes and told her that she could touch his arm if she needed proof he was real.

I kept quiet while she continued. She said she reached out and touched his arm. That's when she realized this was real.

"Who are you?" she asked.

He replied with a question of his own. "Who do I look like?"

Nita said she took a good look at him. "You look like someone I work with. Her name's Terry."

This seemed to agitate the elderly gentleman just a little. "Her name is Theresa, not Terry. She's my daughter and I've been trying to get messages to her, but she isn't hearing me. Tell her I'm around her. Also please tell my granddaughter Theresa to open her eyes and really see what's going on in front of her."

Nita explained that she didn't know how to process all of this. For starters, she didn't understand why my dad didn't know my name was Terry. I told her that the family called me by my full name. My dad never heard the name Terry in relationship to it being my nickname. I also told her the name Theresa meant more to him than the name of his daughter and his granddaughter. My dad would be offended if the full name of Theresa wasn't used, all things considered.

"Am I crazy?" A very honest question asked by a very scared lady.

Of course, I told her no. The message must mean something. Time would reveal its meaning to both me and my daughter. As she turned to leave my office, this sweet woman turned back to looked at me. "Tell your father and all of your Spirits to stay away from me and my home!"

Truthfully I felt bad for Nita. I know all too well about what it's like to suddenly be forced into a "visit" you weren't prepared to have. Honestly, I wished Dad had visited me instead, but if this was the only way he could speak to me, so be it. I was determined to figure out what he was trying to tell me, so I went to see him.

It was a brisk June morning. My next right turn would take me through the arched entrance of the cemetery. Once inside, I drove past the statue of the Blessed Mother then bore left to the parking area. A few construction workers sat on the hillside with their lunches on their laps. Tools and a motor of some sort lay on the ground next to them. I turned off the ignition, grabbed my mace and hopped out of the car.

Whenever my father got excited, or agitated, or surprised he would always yell "Jesus, Mary, and Joseph!" That's the real reason why I had it put on the bottom of his tombstone. Right there at the bottom - all spelled out. Now, when people pay their respect and see it written across the bottom like that they think he's a really holy man.

Dad's new place was at the top of a hill. I put one foot forward when I heard those old familiar words in that old familiar voice.

Jesus, Mary, and Joseph! Theresa! You're here again?

Now, don't get me wrong. I hear voices all day long. It's normal for me, but I still to this day look for reassurance that it's not my imagination. So I glanced over at the tall blond worker in the blue shirt and jeans to see if he heard it too. He nodded his head and took a swig from his water bottle. His partner threw me a quick glance before going back to giving all his attention to what looked like a turkey sandwich. No one else seemed to hear anything.

Why don't you do this for other people?

Well hello to you too Dad, I thought. I speak back telepathically as we are all able to do. Besides the fact that I didn't need everyone in earshot thinking I was a lunatic.

I have no idea what you're talking about, but since it's coming from you, it must mean something important. So by the time I get up to your place, you might as well give me all the answers because I'm going to need a lot of help to understand your message.

Dad explained. *Do this for other people. There are people who can't come here every day. There are people who moved out of state and have loved ones in the cemetery. They can't take them with them. Holidays. Anniversaries. Do nice things for people who can't make it to see their loved ones. Plant flowers. If it snows, clear the snow so the next time the people can come they feel relieved and it's clean for them. You need help too. You could make a little business out of this.*

Look, Dad, I replied. *I'll make a deal with you. I don't have a lot of money but I'll put one ad in the paper. One ad. And if it hits, it hits.*

That night, I went home, sat down at my computer and typed my destiny away. About an hour later, I sat back and read it through one last time.

Cemetery Visitor For Hire

Continue your signs of love and respect for your loved ones who have passed. If you are unable to visit your loved ones for whatever reason, I can help. Whether you need flowers delivered, prayers said or just a status on the condition of the site, I will visit any Westchester or Putnam County cemetery on your behalf. Proof of my visit will be either e-mailed or sent to you through the mail.

I entered my credit card information, said a prayer, and hit submit. One week later, there was a message on my answering machine from a reporter claiming to be from a well-known paper.

"I'd like to speak to you regarding possible representation in our paper at no cost to you. Please return my call at..." He left his return number and said he was looking forward to speaking to me. Me? I must have stared at my phone for a good two minutes. This had to be a mistake. What would the newspaper want with me? I called him back. He answered on the second ring.

"Hi. My name's Theresa. I'm returning your call. I think you called me by mistake. Are you sure you want to speak to me?"

There was a brief pause on the other end and I could hear the shuffle of paper. "Well," he replied, "are you the Cemetery Visitor?"

"Yeah."

"Then yes. I'd like to speak to you."

"May I ask why?"

He explained he works with this photographer that happened to find himself at a rival paper's main headquarters, for the first time ever, the day the issue containing my advertisement came out. He snagged himself a free copy and opened it up to the page that housed my odd little ad. He read it and immediately brought it to his friend who just so happen to be the reporter on the other end of my call.

He continued. "I've already met with my editor and he seems to agree this could be a great human interest story. I have to speak to him again though because right now it's between your story and one other piece."

He let me know he'd be in contact again shortly and the waiting game began. Truthfully, I hoped they picked the other story. God knows I don't need the publicity. Well, technically I did need it. I just really didn't want it. But if this was how things were supposed to play out, then I had to be careful not to allow the media to mention I was a medium. This was something separate from that part of my life. I wanted the cemetery business to garner the respect it deserved and decided not to say a word about being able to communicate with spirit.

Three days later I received my call back from the reporter.

"My editor would like to go with you. When can we meet?"

A few days after that I met with the reporter and his photographer at my local grocer. The florist I worked with had a station there and they wanted to interview her as well.

"Nice to meet you," the reporter smiled. He was a sharp dressed brunette in a business suit. He introduced his photographer who was dressed a bit more casual in khakis and a polo.

My florist was all smiles when she saw us approach. She had on a pretty pink sweater over her usual shirt and apron uniform. Her hair was salon fresh and I could see she was more than excited for her fifteen minutes of fame. After shots were taken and they were done with all the questions, the photographer said he wanted to go down to the riverfront. This was not part of my cemetery routine, but he had a vision of taking pictures of me looking out at the water. Made no sense to me, but this was their article so I obliged.

I sat on a bench at the riverfront patiently waiting for them to set up. The reporter was facing the water doing that square thing with his fingers to try to find the best shot. I turned and looked at the waves. I always love being around running water; water with currency. See, spirits like that kind of energy. They absorb some of it to sustain themselves. I could feel the pull of the spirit that decided to join our party but kept quiet about it. There is a time and place for everything and I felt this was neither the time nor the place. I just sat there quietly, waiting, feeling the pull of the rest of the spirits as they filled their cups.

The photographer tried to take a test shot, but his camera wouldn't work. It simply wouldn't take a photo. I relaxed and waited for him to press all the buttons and pull all the levers to no avail. It didn't bother me that he couldn't get his shot. It wasn't like this riverfront had anything to do with my cemetery visitor business. After several more attempts, he finally threw his hands in the air.

"Damn it," he shouted. "Still won't work right." He shook his head. "It worked fine all morning."

I don't know what got into me just then. Perhaps it was the heat. Perhaps boredom. Either way, the next thing out of my mouth was, "Maybe it's not your fault. Maybe my spirits don't want you to take the picture".

The photographer did not like my joke.

"You know," the reporter let out an uneasy chuckle. "Let's just head over to the cemetery. If you can't get the thing working by the time we're there, we'll have to head back and reschedule."

They had both arrived by train, so instead of them calling a taxi to get to the cemetery, I offered them a ride.

My husband is a realtor and is constantly driving his clients around. You could literally eat off his dashboard, which is why I took his car. I keep the kind of car where you never have to worry about being stranded. You could live out of it for three weeks with all the junk inside.

We piled into his sedan and I hit the button that started up his keyless ignition. This was one of those cars where the key sends a signal to your ignition when it's close. You don't have to take the key out of your pocketbook.

The reporter interviewed me on the way and I think it went well. The photographer sat in the back seat fiddling with his camera. We parked, got out and finished up the interview among the gravestones and flowers. The photographer pulled his camera to his face and tried again. Finally, it worked! He breathed a sigh of relief and started snapping away.

And so it began. We did takes and retakes. It was all about capturing the right moment. They made me do this shot and that shot. Let's show this part of the cemetery and over there too. Walk through the dry leaves, lean against this tree, look this way and that way and that's a wrap.

When all was said and done, we went back to the car and loaded up so I could drive them back to the train station. I hopped in and pushed the button, but the engine didn't kick. I took the key out of my bag and tried again. Nothing.

"Sorry," I said. "I can't get it to start."

The two men in the car looked a bit anxious. I shot the photographer a look through the rearview mirror. "I guess the spirits are here in the cemetery and don't want you to leave."

He didn't even attempt to smile. "That's not funny."

"Okay," I said, "But I've never had a problem starting this car before. Ever."

Either the reporter noticed the photographer was feeling a little uneasy, or he felt it himself because the next thing I know they're both trying to walk me through starting my husband's car. When nothing worked the reporter basically demanded I call my husband since this was obviously a case of driver error.

"What do you mean you can't start the car?" I had my husband on speaker phone. "Theresa, how many times have you driven that thing?"

"I know," I replied. "But I can't start the car. It won't turn on."

He walked me through the same process I had just tried a hundred times. Now the reporter was in the front seat, key in hand, trying to get it to kick over. After a few more tries my husband told me to call him if I couldn't get anywhere and we hung up the phone.

"Now what," the photographer asked.

I snickered. "Wouldn't it be funny if you just admitted you believe in spirits and the car started?"

I watched the color run down his cheeks in the mirror.

"Look, lady," he said in a shaky voice, "I'll admit anything you want right now. All I want to do is get on a train and get the hell out of here."

"Okay," I smiled. "I'm going to take that as you believe in Spirit."

I pushed the button and the engine fired up like a champ. Once we got to the train station - or should I say before we got to the train station. The photographer had the door half open way before I came to a full stop. He tripped over his own two feet, snatched his stuff and took off up the platform two steps ahead of the reporter. Neither of them looked back.

I was surprised they still wanted to do the piece after that, but everything happens for a reason. It was published in the Sunday edition, July 8, 2011, on page seven.

Chapter 8 ½

OLIVIA'S READING

Theresa: My voice becomes severely hoarse indicating that the throat is the trauma area. I feel more as though someone had a tube down their throat and that it's male in energy. I have a male coming through and he makes me feel that he either had a tube down his throat or his throat was his trauma area.

Olivia: Yes, that makes sense. It's my boyfriend.

Theresa: He wants to be acknowledged first. He also wants me to go to the month of October. Does the month of October, the tenth of any month or the number ten mean anything to you?

Olivia: Well that refers to my ex. However, about a year before my boyfriend's passing, we would see the number ten twenty-four keep popping up on the TV screen. So maybe he is referring to that.

Theresa: During my prayer before you arrived, the month of December came up.

Olivia: Yes, that's my dad.

Theresa: I have a mother energy coming through now.

Olivia: Yes, that's my mom.

Theresa: Your boyfriend is now showing me horse stables. I have to figure out why.

Olivia: I really don't know.

Theresa: Okay. He is showing me Northern Westchester regarding the horse stables.

Olivia: That does make sense. I'm a visiting nurse and he would drive me through Northern Westchester. We used to drive past horse stables. But also, my brother's mother-in-law has stables in Northern Westchester.

Theresa: Well your boyfriend is telling you that you will hear news about that family. They never show me bad, but don't chalk it up to coincidence. Your boyfriend is telling me he has been trying to send you signs through coincidences. He also wants you to know that your daughter is gifted. Do you have a daughter?

Olivia: Yes. She's nine years old

Theresa: Is she showing signs of being creative?

Olivia: Yes. She likes to draw.

Theresa: Your boyfriend makes me feel you weren't prepared for his passing. Did he pass suddenly?

Olivia: Yes. He was diagnosed with cancer in March and died in May. I never got to say goodbye to him properly.

Theresa: He wished that he would have died alone. Not because he didn't love you, but he knows you keep playing his death scene over and over in your mind. He was actually out of his body watching you hold his hand. He is also telling me he thought his heart issues would be the cause of death for him.

Olivia: Yes. He did have heart issues, but he didn't die from that.

Theresa: He just brought in the weirdest looking chairs and I have never seen this sign before so bear with me while I figure this out. The chairs are thrones like in a castle.

Olivia: Doesn't make sense to me.

Theresa: He actually is showing me a castle. Besides him thinking he was the head of his castle, did he have a special chair? Not a wheelchair, but maybe a chair no one else would sit in?

Olivia: Only the dining room chair.

Theresa: Nope. He's showing me a more gothic looking chair.

Olivia: I really don't know.

Theresa: Okay. He is mentioning the name Steve. Names can be first, middle, last, or part of the name. For example, Steven can be Mr. Stephenson.

Olivia: Not off hand.

Theresa: Okay. He just wants you to know that there will be an opportunity for you coming through someone with this name.

Olivia: Okay.

Theresa: Now another spirit is coming through and my head is dizzy. Who had either a stroke, Alzheimer, dementia?

Olivia: My grandmother.

Me. She wants to be acknowledged. She wants you to know that things are starting to turn around a little bit.

Olivia: How do you see this stuff?

Theresa: See what?

Olivia: See that this is happening.

Theresa: I don't see it. Part of my prayer before a reading is to keep my mind free so they can put images in my mind. I am just repeating what they're showing me.

Olivia: It is turning around a little bit, but I am afraid it won't go as he wanted it to go.

Theresa: Don't put fear on this. Emotions have energy attached to them as well. Just stay positive. The negative energies can actually affect the event's outcome.

Olivia: Okay.

Theresa: He is putting on these crazy sunglasses. Do you have a picture of him with these sunglasses on?

Olivia: Yes! We took a picture with him wearing these shutter sunglasses. We were on a beach. I have been looking at this picture.

Theresa: See? No such thing as coincidences. He did say that he has been trying to communicate with you using "coincidences". He also wants you to use the word husband when referring to him. He isn't a boyfriend. He says that a boyfriend is a vacation spot. He said he always called you his wife.

Olivia: He did. I wear the ring he bought me as a wedding ring. I always called him my partner, but I will call him my husband.

Theresa: He wants to talk about New York City. What's your connection to the city?

Olivia: My company is based there, but we used to go there a lot.

Theresa: He is asking you to start going there again. He will be with you.

Olivia: Does he visit me at home?

Theresa: Yes. He says you have a birthmark in a weird place.

Olivia: Yes! On my butt!

Theresa: He says your daughter is pure of heart.
Also, he likes the blue stone. Do you know what he
means?

Olivia: Yes. She painted the top of a stone blue and is
now part of the altar we made for him.

Theresa: Is it behind his picture?

Olivia: Yes.

Theresa: Okay. You asked me earlier if he visits you
at home. He just proved that he does. He now is
handing you a jar of pickles. These pickles are cut. Do
you know why?

Olivia: Not really.

Theresa: Okay, well he makes me feel someone
loves pickles.

Olivia: Oh my God! That was me. Every time he had a
sandwich, I would always take his pickles. And they
were always cut!

Theresa: He wants to know about the lawyer.

Olivia: Mine or his?

Theresa: I honestly can't tell.

Olivia: I think it is my lawyer. I'm still going forward
with the divorce from my ex.

Theresa: That doesn't matter to him. He considers you his wife no matter what.

Olivia: Then he is talking about his lawyer pertaining to his son and the school. But I do not have any information yet.

Theresa: He is showing me a safe deposit box.

Olivia: Yes, that makes sense. He gave me money and probably wants me to put it in there instead of where I have it.

Theresa: He is now giving you a hot dog to eat. He is telling me to write him a letter while you are eating. Do you miss meals?

Olivia: Yes.

Theresa: No wonder why he is emphasizing *while* you are eating. He is telling me to tell you it's the crown.

Olivia: The crown?

Theresa: Yes. And he is showing me the king's chair again.

Olivia: Oh my God! Oh my God! I took him down to ████████████ and I have a picture in my phone of him sitting in the King's chair with the crown on! I would have never got to that if he didn't say crown!

Theresa: He wants you to know that he will be with you today.

Olivia: Thank you for everything!

Chapter 9

BACK TO CHURCH

There was a time in my life when I took a little gig at a tombstone company learning to design headstones. One big part of the business was adding names to existing stones. This involved going to the actual tombstone to do pencil rubbings of the lettering on it so they could match the size and font. I knew cemeteries well. I've always loved being in cemeteries and often took walks on nice days. Since I knew them well, it was my job to go out and rub them. This was a perfect gig for me.

I went to work, received my assignments and was off to the cemeteries. I arrived back to the office and went inside. When you first walk into the office there's a hallway that leads to the front desk. In the hall stands a beautiful statue of the Virgin Mother. I stood admiring it when a woman that worked in the office walked by. We got to chatting a while when a spirit appeared to me with a message for her.

"You're going to think I'm crazy, but…"

I relayed the message.

She immediately demanded I tell her how I knew that. Her comment served as my clarity.

I took a few minutes to tell her a little about myself and my ability to communicate with Spirit. She scoffed and told me she was Roman Catholic and didn't believe in "that stuff". I could have fired back with a "So am I!" But I didn't. Well, technically I couldn't since she abruptly turned on her heels and walked away.

It reminded me of the first time I met Nita. Maybe she'd come around. Or maybe she wouldn't. Heck. Maybe she was right. Maybe what I was doing went against the faith like everyone always told me. Maybe they were all right. But deep down inside I knew they were wrong - every last one of them.

I stopped going to church after my daughter received her confirmation back in ninety-eight. According to Catholic Doctrine, I was technically excommunicated after my first divorce. However, that wasn't the reason I didn't go. As a matter of fact, I always wanted to go. I wanted to do what I was taught was right, but something - anything really - always came up. Either I had a headache or needed to wash my hair or stubbed my toe or blah blah blah.

I don't really know what kept me away from church. I wasn't mad at God. That wasn't what kept me away. There was a point in my life when I hid my gifts. I didn't want people to know what I did. All my life I was judged for my gift. A gift God gave me. I guess it was starting to get to me. Maybe this was wrong. What if I was fooled by the devil and he was using me to do his evil work? Problem with that theory is I couldn't find anything evil in the messages I gave. Nothing was ever bad. It brought people relief. How could that be evil? It didn't make sense. I knew in my heart where my gift came from. I knew in my heart it was good. But was it wrong? Here I was about to embark on a brand new venture. My name was in the limelight. Things were happening because of my gifts and I still couldn't make up my mind about the whole thing. But since the message came from my soul mate, I knew I had to have faith.

Then came that random Sunday. Out of the blue, I woke up with an instant pull to go to church. Today had to be the day. I knew it in my soul. And I had to be at the twelve o'clock mass. I knew that as well. Honestly, though I had the pull, I didn't have the drive. I didn't really want to go. But I followed my gut, grabbed my nice blue suit jacket, threw on another coat of hairspray and reluctantly dragged my tukus to church.

Churches are works of art with their stone structures and wood features. I found an empty pew in the back out of the way of other people. I sat down to admire the stained glass windows before service began and I'd have to sit, kneel, stand, kneel, sit, kneel… well, you get it.

I glanced at the cross in the center of the room and thought, *Well, I'm here. Show me why, please.*

Out walked an old father, robes crystal clean and perfectly hung, He approached the podium and began today's sermon.

John 20:24-29 New International Version (NIV)

Jesus Appears to Thomas

24 Now Thomas, one of the Twelve, was not with the disciples when Jesus came.
25 So the other disciples told him, "We have seen the Lord!"
But he said to them, "Unless I see the nail marks in his hands and put my finger where the nails were, and put my hand into his side, I will not believe."
26 A week later his disciples were in the house again, and Thomas was with them. Though the doors were

locked, Jesus came and stood among them and said, "Peace be with you!"

27 Then he said to Thomas, "Put your finger here; see my hands. Reach out your hand and put it into my side. Stop doubting and believe."

28 Thomas said to him, "My Lord and my God!"

29 Then Jesus told him, "Because you have seen me, you have believed; blessed are those who have not seen and yet have believed."

Service was over shortly after and, since I was closest to the door, I was the first one out. I heard the sermon but didn't fully understand the message. Perhaps this was going to be my 'Aha!' moment.

An 'Aha!' moment is when a message doesn't make sense right away. Then suddenly, one day, something happens and you go "Aha! That's what the message meant!" I decided not to worry about it anymore now. I was too busy to think about it, anyway.

Once the article printed and word got out, my phone wouldn't stop ringing. A lot of people showed interest or were morbidly curious and full of questions. Then there was the other reporter.

"We'd like to talk to you about doing a human interest piece," this guy said. "We can meet whenever and wherever you'd like."

"Are you sure you want to talk to me," I replied. "Someone just did one."

"Are you Theresa Marotta?"

"Yes," I replied.

"Then yes," he replied. "We'd also like to do a piece on you."

Turns out this guy was from a very small novelty press, but any press is good press, so they say. I had to go along for the ride away. I had to trust *them*. So I made another appointment for another interview for another article.

Chapter 9 ½

TESTIMONIAL OF A CCD TEACHER

I had my first reading with Terry in 2012 and it was amazing. She picked up on things no one else had ever brought to light, but what was so amusing about that first read was when she asked, "What's with you and chipmunks?" I had noticed so many of them in my yard and running across my driveway that afternoon that I told my husband to make sure they couldn't get into the basement or the house.

Since then I've had many readings - each one always amazing. One time I was directed to a key in the drawer that I didn't know was there. I sent a picture of it to Terry along with the explanation of what it was. I have had numerous messages from loved ones. For me it always helps.

About a year or so ago Terry announced she was having classes and I jumped at the chance. I've always had an interest in the metaphysical and I am an extremely spiritual person; not religious. I have been to more than my share of card readers and physics and got to the point where I could read my own cards.

As my classes progressed and my gifts developed,

I told Terry how I teach CCD. She asked how do you do that when your beliefs are not in line with Catholic Doctrine? She knows the issues I have with the hierarchy of the church organization. I said I take the lessons in that book and I apply it to the kid's lives. I now teach eighth grade. I have had my class since fifth grade. I am giving them life lessons and letting them know how much God, the Blessed Mother, and Jesus truly loves them. I can't teach them what I believe in because it is not according to church doctrine.

My son is a student in my class. Sometimes, when we get home after class, he'll look at me and ask why I don't tell the class about my gifts and spirituality like I've told and taught my children. I explained why I can't. I was surprised because most of the time I feel he tunes me out. I asked him why he thought I should teach that, anyway. He said, "well because it's more interesting than what's in the book and when you talk about that 'stuff' I can see how much you love Jesus and all the 'invisible friends' as you call them".

You have an angel for everything and maybe the kids can use them the way you taught me to. So I took his advice and on the feast day of the Archangels this year we talked about all the Archangels, even the ones not in the Bible, and all the realms. I gave homework that they go home and find an angel that they can relate to. It was one of the best classes we ever had. I do have to watch what I say and bite my tongue at times even when I am in mass.

My kids will laugh because they see how annoyed I get during the homilies. I heard about a very young new priest who told the church they should go up shaking to receive. Then stated, "even if you cannot receive communion, come up with your arms crossed in front of you and I will bless you".

Oh really? So after I admit I'm a sinner and walk through my Father's house shaking you're going to bless me? Are you kidding with that?

I know I don't need to be afraid of God and I don't need to be shaking when I receive communion. I don't need you standing there in judgment of someone who cannot receive. So yes, I have issues with the church, but not my faith!

There's a great quote: Spirituality doesn't need religion, but religion needs spirituality.

Sincerely,

Dawn

Chapter 10

THE COW IS PURPLE

Another article hit the newsstands. Now reporters were calling from television stations. We met. We filmed. They interviewed me. They asked questions about my religion. I explained I wasn't religious, but spiritual. Article after article, paper after paper, channel after channel. As time went on, I became less and less subtle about my gifts and spirituality.

I told one television reporter about the Lady in White and how no one else could see her. She asked me for more stories so I told her about the time I was walking in the cemetery and thought I heard a cat crying. I followed the noise to a grave of a little boy who was born and passed in the same year. What I thought was a cat was a tiny child crying. I put a flower on his grave and said a little prayer and the crying stopped. She asked how I was able to hear him and I explained I was an energist - a person who can read energy. Then I explained that I was not a carnival psychic.

Carnival psychic's have more adornments than abilities; crystal balls, magic mirrors, beads. They speak in very general terms. They may say things like, "You'll find love". They will also try to upsell you by telling you there's a curse on you and they can remove it thus creating dependency. I'm no carnival psychic.

I appeared on a couple of news programs. Then I went viral. I was all over the internet. People blogged about me. People dissected the articles about me into a million pieces. My face ended up on opinion websites and you know what they say about opinions. Are you Pro? Are you Con? Is it right? Is it wrong? Would you do it? Do you believe in life after death? Do you believe there are those who can communicate? Is it sacrilegious? Would it bother you if it was?

There were the pros:

"We live out of state. It would be great if someone checked in for us."

"This would be great for my father. He waters my mother's plants every day, but will be away for a month."

There were those that thought it was a waste of money even though I only charged $25 per visit. Think about gas prices nowadays. I wasn't exactly paying the rent with my earnings.

There were atheists that ranted about how it didn't matter because life after death didn't exist.

"Doesn't matter. I'll be dead and that's it."

There were family members that argued they wouldn't want their lazy next of kin sending replacements. Some man on the internet said I could go visit anyone I wanted to in his family and in the future I could go visit him because according to him, I was easy on the eyes. That one made me cringe.

"I would never forgive my lazy *** family if they sent a stranger to my grave."

And there were the religious ones who couldn't get past the "psychic" thing. Here I was again in the line of fire being judged for what I was, who I was and what I could do.

"She does the devil's work. She's going to hell."

"What a shame because she really is helping people. "I pray for her soul."

Pray for my soul? My soul? Really? Look, lady, I just so happen to have a personal relationship with the Man upstairs and his Mother. I'm pretty sure we're good. At least I hope so. A comment like that used to bring the Bronx Italian right out of me. I would have put up a good fight and told her all about her religion. But I didn't. It isn't my place to tell people what to think. I learned that lesson in my late thirties.

There was a time in the nineties when I developed a bit of an ego. I had this holier than thou attitude about religion. I mean, I saw heaven, so my way of thinking was the one true way, right? Wrong. I learned that in a dream.

I remember laying in bed one night in REM state (dream state) when the Blessed Mother appeared to me. In a flash, we were in a conference room, Her by my side. There wasn't anyone else in the room.

Before me was a conference table with one chair on each side. A vase of roses had been placed in the middle. For some reason I had that feeling I used to get when I was called to the principal's office and I didn't know why yet, but I wasn't afraid of whatever was about to happen.

The Blessed Mother told me to choose my own seat. I could sit on any side except the head of the table. I chose the chair on the left. She told me to look at the table and describe what I saw.

No way the answer could be this easy. It confused me. "Roses?"

She asked me how many roses. I didn't know if I was allowed to count them so I quickly spit out "Six?"

She told me to move to one of the chairs at the head of the table and sit down. Again, She told me to describe what I saw, but this time she granted permission to count the roses. I sat in a different chair at the same table and looked at the same vase. There appeared to be quite a few more than last time. I counted carefully. "Eighteen."

When She had me sit in the third chair, the vase was stuffed. When I got to the fourth and final chair She held her hand out and told me to place my own within Hers. I was afraid to hold Her hand. I thought, if I did, certain death would follow. Why else would She ask for my hand other than to take me to some place I may or may not want to be? Even while I was having my doubts, I found my hand went inside Hers. I was afraid, but I trusted Her.

Suddenly we were hovering over the vase still in the conference room. She asked me to count the roses. I looked down and quickly realized it was an impossible task. There were way too many roses to count. They were everywhere.

After what felt like an eternity I found myself sitting back in the first chair I started in - about six roses in the vase in front of me.

The Virgin Mother asked me what I learned. I had no idea. But I didn't want to tell Her that. The only answer I could think of was that it had to do with one's own perspective. I admit I'm not a smart person. I told Her I needed help.

She explained. "These roses represent the religions of the world. Say I tell one rose to believe a cow is purple. I tell another to believe a cow is red. I tell others it is polka dotted. In the end, does it really matter what the true color of the cow is? What matters is that you have the faith to believe, beyond all doubt in the color of *your* cow."

This concept was further backed up with a personal example. She asked what my children call me. I love easy questions!

"Mom," I smiled. Then She asked what my family calls me. Then my friends. After I gave her all three names She smiled beautifully.

"You see? It doesn't matter what people call you. You are still the same person. So when people refer to my Son as Jesus or Emmanuel or Jehovah or Allah or by any other name, is He not still the same person? You must stop judging the different religions of the world as they each hold a piece of the true color of the picture."

I took this message to heart and have carried it with me all these years. It doesn't matter to me if you're my religion, another religion, made up your own religion, chose not to have a religion; I honestly don't care what you believe as long as you're a good person. In the end that's really all that matters. And always keep an open mind.

(The following reading is a great example of what happens when you don't.)

Chapter 10 ½

DONNA'S READING

Theresa: Do you suffer with anxiety?

Donna: Yes.

Theresa: The anxiety is here right away. So they put a red stone near you. Now, you know, colors have their own energy and red is the color of rebirth, so I know you're connected to the other side. Now, it could also be literal. Does the month of January or July mean anything to you?

Donna: July. My father's birthday was in July.

Theresa: He's passed.

Donna: Yes.

Theresa: He's the first one that wants to come in.

Donna: I welcome him in.

Theresa: Now the month of November is here. What's the month of November or the eleventh of any month?

Donna: November is my parents anniversary and the eleven - my mother had a thing for eleven eleven.

Theresa: Is she on the other side?

Donna: Yes.

Theresa: Okay. That's why. Dad brings in Mom. So it's the anniversary. That's how he brings her in. What's with your stomach? Are you having digestive problems? Or are certain foods bothering you because he's a little concerned about your stomach? It's going to be food related. They don't show me bad so this isn't going to be bad. Dad is trying to tell me you're going to develop a sensitivity to certain foods. Because you're getting deeper. Do you do cards? How do you relate to them? He makes me feel like you relate to them almost on a daily basis.

Donna: Yes.

Theresa: How do you do that?

Donna: Um, he sends me signs. I talk to them and they send me signs.

Theresa: So he's right. And it's not a coincidence that he comes in first.

Donna: No. Not at all.

Theresa: He's the strongest one for you.

Donna: Oh yeah.

Theresa: Who was in the medical field or wanted to be a nurse or EMT? I work in a hospital, nursing home, it's the same energy. And this one your father is holding steady with.

Donna: Someone I know that was a nurse or a doctor?

Theresa: Or wanted to be a nurse because he puts the medical field near you. So if you're bringing in the energy - if I'm not a nurse or a doctor, I work in a doctor's office. Did you want to be in the medical field at some point?

Donna: I'm a psychotherapist.

Theresa: There ya go. You're in the medical field for me. That's why he puts it near you. That's how simple this is. That's just his confirmation. Now, because you're highly developed in your brain, I want you to put that to the side. We're just going with gut feelings. See? You're smiling now. Now you're more relaxed. Okay. Now we do it. Who was left handed or does something with their left hand?

Donna: Dead or alive?

Theresa: I don't know. See, when I don't see someone and your father is putting the image in my mind, I don't know.

Donna: My children's father was left handed. He was the only one.

Theresa: Is he on the other side or is he living?

Donna: He's alive.

Theresa: Okay good. See, this is my veil. Anything here *Theresa points left* is on the other side, anything here *Theresa points right* is living. If they mention a name, or they put an image or a person, I can't be a hundred percent sure. That's why I can't see him. You're going to hear news about him. You still hold energy with him.

Donna: Yes.

Theresa: There's still a connection, other than the children. Your father is saying, 'Other than the children, there's still a connection there'.

Donna: I mean, we made two children together and I raise one of his kids. It's not about kids?

Theresa: No. It's not about the kids. Unless what you're doing is residual. You know about residual energy. I'm touching this wall. My energy is here. Right now there's residual energy there. Energy doesn't just disappear, so its residual energy.

Donna: Okay.

Theresa: There's residual energy coming from him to you. Doesn't have to do with the kids. That's current. You're still carrying around scars from him. Are you in constant contact? Do you contact him other than for the kids? Your father's telling me there's residual energy there.

Donna: We're all worried about him because he's getting older.

Theresa: For health problems?

Donna: Eh, no. His brain, but...

Theresa: There you go. So you're having…

Donna *interrupts*: My father isn't guiding me about him!

Theresa: He wants to give you a message about him. That's all he wants to do. You're going to hear something about him. You may want to get involved in it, to help out, but don't. That's all. All this was for that.

Donna: But don't?

Theresa: But don't. It's a problem that doesn't have anything to do with the kids. If he says to you, listen we have a problem with this one, then yes, those are your kids. But your father is talking about energy that has nothing to do with the kids. He's showing me a brick building. So when - the Archangel Michael just came in. That's cool. I'll go there in a minute. Now, when I see a brick building, either it's literally someone lives in a brick building, or someone's getting involved in real estate. It could be either I'm selling something, I'm buying something. Why would Dad show me a brick building?

Donna: My aunt lived in a brick building.

Theresa: They're either going to come in showing me memories or a current event in order to stay. You're wearing the Archangel Michael's color.

Donna: Oh I am?

Theresa: The purple is Archangel Michael. Now.
when he shows up even that's not a coincidence.
First, you need to start calling him to you for
protection. It's very easy. Just call him.

There are three colors that are responsible for
protection. It comes from Archangel Michael. Picture
three hula hoops. You need to do it. Someone like
you, you need to do the hula hoops. You deal with
heavy energies in your profession. Depression is a
heavy energy. Alcoholism is a heavy energy. Drugs.
Heavy energy is not just evil; its heavy energy. So
picture the hula hoop furthest away from you is
purple. When Archangel Michael deals with heavy
energies he slays, or cuts into it with his sword, the
aura from his sword turns purple. Anything the
Archangel Michael allows to come in is going to be
okay. It's not going to be heavy.

Donna: Okay.

Theresa: The next hula hoop they have to get through
is green. Green is always healing. Green is Archangel
Raphael. Once it comes through Archangel Michael
and through Archangel Raphael it has to pass through
the white - which is the closest one to you. That's the
light. So it starts from protection, to healing, to the
light. These three colors. That's why Archangel
Michael showed up. Were you thinking of doing
cards? Did you go to a card reader? Because
Archangel Michael is putting Angel cards near you.
Start asking him to help you on a path.

Donna: Okay.

Theresa: This is what they're showing me. You're steady here and there's a possibility here and a possibility here. Both of these possibilities are good but one is better than the other. So they'll guide you there. There's going to be a decision soon that you have to make. It could be as simple as do I want to move my office? Or do I want to expand this? But it's good. It's all good for you. Are you remembering your dreams because you're very active in your dream state they make me feel?

Donna: Yes.

Theresa: Do you wake up exhausted sometimes?

Donna: Yes.

Theresa: So let me tell you what's going on with this. It's your father that wants you to know he's working with Archangel Michael with you. Now when you wake up and you're tired that just means the soul went back to get recharged. Like a battery to a cell phone. Sometimes what happens is the soul is not fully immersed as we're waking up. So we may feel pressure. We may feel paralyzed. We may feel scared like we had a demon or negative something sitting on our chests and couldn't breathe (Old Hag Syndrome). No. It just means that you were waking up before the soul was fully immersed. I have a gentleman on the other side. I did not die naturally. Unfortunately he's going to bring in these friggin strays. "I'm not a stray", he's saying.

Donna: He's not.

Theresa: He's saying he's not. He wants you to know he's in a better place and there's a thank you and an apology coming up from this person. Does that make any sense to you?

Donna: Yes.

Theresa: He wants to thank you first, not apologize first. For him, it doesn't work the other way around. I want to thank you first so there's validation there first. And then there's admittance. Now, he's been around you for a while you know.

Donna: Yes.

Theresa: I see a black jacket. So even colors mean something to me. Do you have a black suit jacket?

Donna: I don't wear suits.

Theresa: A blazer. See black is your power color. Black is not negative, its power. But your father says you know a lot of things that are going on and you're not recording them, meaning writing them down. And you have to, because when you deal with that side, because they're the mirror image of us so they give us the answers first and we have to figure out the questions.

Donna: Okay.

Theresa: Here, we ask questions, we like to get an answer. You're getting all these answers you don't know what the hell the questions were. Now, I need to tell you you're going to be doing this for a living also.

Donna: Oh dear.

Theresa: In a healing way. It's not going to be one on one like I do. It's more like a group therapy situation. You'll be able to put the spirituality with the scientific. That's what I mean by doing that.

Donna: I already do that.

Theresa: That's what I'm talking about. It going to grow. That might be one of the decisions coming up. Am I going do it more? Am I going to do it in another location? It's going to be that kind of thing. That's what you're supposed to be doing as well. Unlike an individual patient doctor relationship.

Donna: Oh.

Theresa: So you know the difference between a dream and a visit.

Donna: I do.

Theresa: Okay. So you remember the visits.

Donna: I haven't had too many, but I know them.

Theresa: The visits you will always remember until the day that you die.

Donna: Yes.

Theresa: You're going to get more of those visits. But the problem with you is that you're not recording them. So, what you need to do when you remember it, wake up, put the date and write what you remember. Then don't even look at it. That's an answer. You could look at it three weeks later or so and then you find your question. And you'll find your question through a coincidence. Do you know a Jerry, Jeremy, something like that. Okay. This Jerry/Jeremy is coming to you. This may be a new patient that needs help. Your father is saying his name. When you hear about Jerry, Jeremy or you get a new patient it's not a coincidence. He needs more healing spiritually, then he needs mentally.

Donna: Okay. I'll keep my ears out for him.

Theresa: You won't have to. He's going to find you. I'm very nervous. Who suffers with severe anxiety or anxiousness? But it's almost like I don't want to take a step out, like agoraphobic, where it actually hinders me to take the next step.

Donna: My mom comes the closet as someone who is like that.

Theresa: Okay. Who's artistic? She's artistic. I'm creative. Whose very creative? So I could be musically inclined, music is therapy. What is she talking about? Okay. Who listens to a lot of music because they're able to tune out the world. It's more therapeutic for me.

Donna: Out of everyone, I listen to the most music.

Theresa: Is it more, therapeutic for you than enjoyment. I want to listen to it and I can drown everything else out.

Donna: Okay.

Theresa: If the answer's "okay" then it's not you. You have another artistic side to you, so I have to figure out what your mother is telling me. Either I can write very well, I can paint, I have a good rapport with color, I know how to place things.

Donna: Could be anything. I write. I used to make jewelry that was the beads. You said something about beads when I first walked in.

Theresa: Oh and the beads. That's why. There you go, artistic. That's what she's talking about. Do you still do that?

Donna: No.

Theresa: Oh, you should go back to it. The jewelry. Was it only beads that you did?

Donna: Mostly I worked with beads.

Theresa: Okay. So that's with the beads? Your decision making should be during the evening when the moon is out. Not during the day. That's when you can make your decisions. She's holding a baby. Did someone have a miscarriage, or the baby wasn't able to be born?

Donna: Everybody has a miscarriage.

Theresa: It's a little boy. It's blood to her. We'll just leave it. She doesn't want to leave it. It was a stillborn. Who had the stillborn? You'll find out because it's on mom's side because its mom holding the baby.

Donna: Nobody had a stillborn.

Theresa: Because I see the baby born. I could have been five six months pregnant. I see the baby. I don't see the fetus. But I have to leave it there. Because she's holding it.

Donna: Maybe I have the wrong pencil again.

Theresa: No because your mother started with the beads and started with the jewelry again. But for someone who's gypsy like… How did you know you were a gypsy, and what do you mean when I say gypsy?

Donna: *giggles* Well my father's Romanian. And we always joked that there's a gypsy side to us. And um, I've only been to one other reading and the lady said I don't need to be there as I could do this myself.

Theresa: Except that dad makes me feel like you just need clarity to that. That you know you have the ability, you just need clarity to it. See he gives me the answers first I have to figure out the questions. Crossing the two worlds the spiritual and the scientific, have you been doing that awhile?

Donna: I just tried it to keep my parents close to me but that's it.

Theresa: But he makes me feel about the business. How long ago did you try?

Donna: It's been a part of my practice for a long time.

Theresa: Good. Because that is what you're meant to be doing. One foot here and one foot on the other side. The problem is you didn't know how to discern or protect. Dad wants to make sure you know that he is working with the Archangel Michael and just visualize the three hula hoops and you'll be fine. So he's going into this swimming pool. I have to figure out why.

Donna: That was a big part of our lives, the swimming pool.

Theresa: Okay. They keep it very simple for me. That's a memory. That's the only reason why he's doing it. What do you have that's green in the office? Do you have green candles? A green wall? Because green is healing. You have to have the green in your office.

Donna: There's nothing green in my office.

Theresa: Then can you get a candle or something green?

Donna: Sure.

Theresa: I have a woman coming through. And someone else was big into jewelry because I hear her coming before she gets here. So I'm wearing either a lot of bangles, charms. I'm not mom. And I'm heavier than you. I have more meat on my bones. She also likes the other color green which is August. Why is she bringing up August? Now that could be August or the eighth of any month. The eight is near you. Plus, you know eight is infinity.

Donna: I've never thought about it like that but you're right. Hm. I don't know that many people who passed.

Theresa: She's chunky. And she's coming in more towards mom. If they come in near one particular parent over the other than "I come in through mom's family". I liked my bracelets. I liked it. And I heard her coming before, and she's telling me the eight or the August. Was someone's birthday in August? Did someone pass in August? Or the number eight.

Donna: No. Nobody passed in August. Nobody passed on the eighth.

Theresa: Because that's another green month. It's a healing month for me. Or the infinity. Do you have the sign of infinity?

Donna: No.

Theresa: I don't know. I have to be honest with you. For someone who's so open to them…

Donna: Oh, I'm very open to them.

Theresa: They showed me that the moment you walked through my door. You might deal with them differently than I deal with them.

Donna: Yeah.

Theresa: Do you know what I mean?

Donna: No.

Theresa: They speak to us very intimately. When they speak to me they give me *my* signs. They may give you different signs. So they're speaking to me in my signs. One of the most important signs that you cannot disregard is Archangel Michael. That you can't disregard.

Donna: Okay.

Theresa: This young guy keeps trying to come through. But to me you're closed off.

Donna: No. Not at all.

Theresa: Not to them. To them you're open. But I can't go passed your eyes right now.

Donna: I don't know why.

Theresa: I don't know why either. It's not that you're purposely doing it.

Donna: I know I want to know. I really want to know.

Theresa: Okay. So they gave me some clarity, with the dreams. You have to start writing them down. You know about the coincidences because that's how they speak.

Donna: I know.

Theresa: Your father doesn't use the birds. Who said he uses the birds as symbols? Birds isn't his thing.

Donna: No.

Theresa: That's what he's saying. There's a cat here though. And the cat is a spirit cat. It's not a live cat.

Donna: Okay.

Theresa: You're more intuitive than psychic. Intuitive is I can deal more with *them*. Don't come to me to tell you my future.

Donna: Oh I'd like to know the future. Can you do that?

Theresa: Yes. But you need to go to more of a psychic. I'm more intuitive with *them*.

Donna: Well if they have something to tell me, I'm totally open.

Theresa: That's what Dad was trying to tell you, to lay down the groundwork to develop this gift that you have. And as you develop it, with the writing down of what you remember and recognizing your coincidences, you have to learn how to protect yourself. Why is he showing me this big boat?

Donna: That's my dad.

Theresa: I don't know why he is showing me this.

Donna: He had a big boat.

Theresa: Oh. He had.

Donna: I think that my dad is here because what you said about July, the swimming pool, the big boat. That's my dad.

Theresa: Okay. Archangel Michael to protect his daughter.

Donna: That means nothing to me to be honest.

Theresa: It's what Archangel Michael provides. It's not the person himself. And Archangel Michael is not a religious...

Donna: Oh I know. I know about angels.

Theresa: Oh. Okay. He's trying to teach you how to discern because you're letting in other spirits. Do you know what I mean?

Donna: No.

Theresa: You can let in spirits because you're intuitive. You have the "Open For Business" sign on for *them*. So you have to be careful who you let through the door. You can set up the rules because you have control over them. They don't have control. He wanted you to understand why some times when you wake up you're exhausted because your soul leaves to...

Donna: I know. I'm very busy at night.

Theresa: Yeah.

Donna: See, I dream.

Theresa: But you're not recording it and you're not looking back at it.

Donna: It would be impossible to record. I have too many dreams. I mean I dream all night long.

Theresa: Me too. Do you fly?

Donna: No. I haven't flown in a long time. I mean, I've done it, but I haven't flown in a long time.

Theresa: Okay. Are you able to…

Donna: *interrupts* I know that my dad is here, but what is it that he wants me to know? If he's here with the pool, with the boat, with the August. I already know that he's here. What does he want to tell me?

Theresa: Okay. This is what's important to him, right now. *points to the paper*. It's branching off. This is growth.

Donna: Okay.

Theresa: Don't get involved with the ex when you have nothing to do with it. He wants you to learn to discern between spirits. Even before you go to sleep. Do you dream of the water?

Donna: Sometimes.

Theresa: Are you master of the water or do you drown in the water?

Donna: I never drown.

Theresa: What is the color of the water?

Donna: I don't know. Most of my dreams are not water based. I've dreamt of water before.

Theresa: They are going to start becoming water based. And this is water that has currency to it. And with the currency comes the electrical energy that they need. Because they're energy right now. In a couple of days it'll make more sense to you because they give you the answers first and you have to figure out what the questions are.

Donna: What are the answers you're giving me Terry. I'm so confused.

Theresa: The answers are first, you are on your path, but there's growth there. Are you stopping yourself from branching off? Don't do that. That's what your father is trying to tell you. Don't be preoccupied with the past, which is the ex.

Donna: I'm not preoccupied with him at all. My god it's been a billion years we've had no contact. I told you that.

Theresa: Okay. He's showing some residual energy there. You may want to help him and your father is saying no. This is the central thing; you have this opportunity and this opportunity. But you have to do one at a time. Why are you hesitate for the growth?

Donna: I'm not.

Theresa: Where's the opportunity for the growth. This is what he's talking about. A special flower.

Donna: My mother's favorite flower was orchid. My favorite flower is hydrangea. By aunt was cactus before she died.

Theresa: Your aunt. Your aunt. Hold on. Was she heavy?

Donna: Yeah.

Theresa: There you go.

Donna: It's not her. If you can tell me why you think it's her because she didn't wear jewelry. I mean she didn't wear big bangles. You wouldn't have heard her before she came into a room.

Theresa: Okay because I see the heaviness in the arms. Do you wear a lot of bracelets?

Donna: No.

Theresa: Then I don't know. I saw the heavy arm the minute you mentioned her. Let me give you... do you want the name of a psychic? Because psychics can tell you more or less what's going on and what's going to go on. Oh, what's your connection to New Jersey?

Donna: I don't have one.

Theresa: Okay. Because there's money coming in from Jersey. There's a connection coming from Jersey. Do you want me to give you the name of a psychic?

Donna: Yes.

Theresa: *Pulls out business card for psychic that has a picture of angel wings on it*: The wings. You know, and I would think of the infinity.

Donna: And the colors you told me about. *points to the card* The green, the purple and the white.

Theresa: There you go. I didn't even realize that. Isn't that funny?

Chapter 11

BENITA'S FINAL MESSAGE

I wasn't the only one that stopped working at the flooring store. Nita left. She had to. She was ill; too ill to work. She explained this when she called, out of the blue, shortly after I returned to church.

"Your father came to see me again," she said.

"Look," I apologized. "I truly have zero control over that. I keep telling him to come to me with my messages and leave you out, but they do what they want. So what was my message this time?"

"The message wasn't for you," she explained.

She said my father appeared to her and told her her father would come visit her. He told her she shouldn't speak to him. If she did, he would take her to the other side, but not in an evil or malicious way. In the way one would imagine a father would help his daughter crossover. My father explained to her it wasn't her time yet. He said she could refuse for now. He told her she was at a crossroads and could choose.

Nita said she got very sick and went to the hospital. They told her she was suffering kidney and liver failure. Her condition went from bad to "She has about thirty-four minutes to live."

She said all she remembered after that was feeling awful then drifting away. Her father appeared to her in her dream. He held out his arms to embrace her.

She smiled and shook her head no. He smiled back and disappeared. Back on earth, our plane, they had located a donor. Organs were on their way. They arrived just in time for the doctors to perform her life-saving surgery. She called to tell me she was alive and well - for now. It was the closest to acceptance I would ever feel.

Nita still calls occasionally. We chit chat about this and that; catch up. She never speaks about my gifts or what happened in the past. But I know that deep down inside she no longer condemns me for my abilities and has seen the good that can come from them.

Two years after I went back to church I received another random phone call. This time it was from the Roman Catholic woman I worked with at the tombstone company.

"I need to talk to you. In person."

I asked if everything was all right. She said yes, but reiterated that she "just needed to talk to me". I met her on Central Avenue.

We sat down at a small restaurant and ordered lunch.

She began with, "You know, I've been praying for your soul."

Here we go again, I thought. "Oh yeah, why?"

She replied, "Because I thought you were doing the devil's work. That's what I'm taught to believe. I know you're going to think I'm crazy, but Jesus Christ Himself told me to leave you alone. He said you're doing His work."

The church sermon came flooding back into my mind. Jesus had to appear to Thomas - doubting

Thomas because Thomas said he wouldn't believe it was Jesus unless he could put his hands inside his wounds.

Jesus appeared to him and allowed Thomas to touch his wounds. After he did, Thomas fell to the ground and knew it was true. Jesus told him blessed are those that don't need the proof. This was my sign. The day God called me back to church he chose to speak about how people saw Jesus after he died. It was possible. It was true. Even the good book references it. They saw Jesus after death. His believers could speak to his energy after it passed just like I can do now. God sent me a message that what I was doing was all right. He gave me His blessing to continue. I thanked Him for His message and decided to make performing readings a full-time job.

With God on my side and the help of my soul friends and mates, both here and from beyond the veil, I promised to relay as many messages to as many people as fate will allow. I don't plan on stopping anytime soon. I even did a reading for my Roman Catholic friends almost entire family. We have a mutual respect for each other now.

Lets fast forward a few more years.

September, 2018. One night I have this vivid dream; the type of dream one doesn't forget. Instead it repeats in your head for days. I sat on this dream for two full weeks because there was a message in it. The message was for someone else and I really didn't want to give this certain someone a message. Not that it was bad. On the contrary, it was a wonderful message. I just wasn't sure if Father Kenny would appreciate it.

Father Kenny performed the twelve o'clock mass on Sundays. I began going to the five o'clock mass on

Saturday in order to avoid feeling compelled to pass this one message along. Imagine my surprise months later when Father Kenny walked out and began five o'clock mass one Saturday afternoon.

I sat in my pew in the very back of the church arguing with God in my head. I did not want to relay this message. What if he condemned me and threw me out of church? I argued during the entire service yet still ended up waiting outside on the stairs when mass was over. I watched the crowd disperse. Out walks Father Kenny to greet those church members that remained. I stood patiently waiting for everyone to leave. If I had to relay this message I really didn't want or need an audience, but sure enough, there he goes asking if I needed help.

"I had a dream Father," I explained. "There was a new priest performing mass. He did it totally different than you do. He had the whole place up and dancing. Even I was dancing and I don't dance in church. He was a good looking guy too. Long light brown wavy hair; green/blue eyes like the water in Aruba. I thought it was such a waste," I let out an uneasy chuckle.

"This was a dream, right?" He asked. I couldn't help but notice we had the attention of everyone that hadn't left the church yet, which was now quite a few people forming a semicircle around us.

"Yes," I continued. There is a time during Catholic mass when the priest does a blessing on the crowd with holy water using a tool called an aspergillum. He uses this ball on stick tool to spray water onto the crowd. I explained to Father Kenny during the blessing of the water the water defied gravity. Instead of going out onto the crowd it flew way up into the air. In order to receive the blessing we had to put our palms out above our heads. The droplets landed on each outstretched palm in the same place where the nails were driven through Jesus' hands.

I continued. "I left and went outside. There was a snowstorm and I was having trouble finding my white car in the snow. There was too much of it. I continue to walk down the street and this new priest is chasing after me yelling he needs to speak to me. Finally I turned around. 'Can I help you?' I asked him." I mean, he was good looking, but too young for me. I didn't tell Father Kenny this part of the dream. I also didn't tell him the priest in my dream gently grabbed and held me by my right wrist.

"The new priest said, 'tell Father Kenny I love the way he loves me'. In the dream I was still in the snow, cold and not knowing where my car was so I was annoyed. I asked him who he was. He just smiled and disappeared."

I knew who he was when I woke up. It was Jesus. That's why He held mass like no other. That's why His water went to heaven to be blessed before falling back to earth onto our palms like that.

I ended the story and waited. Father Kenny wasted no time. He grabbed me by my right wrist in the exact manner in which Jesus had in my dream. "You just made every hair on my body stand up," he said. And that's when it happened. Father Kenny began to give me my own blessing.

Now let me explain what a private blessing truly means to a Catholic. In my faith there is less than a handful of times you are ever blessed alone. During your Baptism, shortly after birth, during your last rites, shortly before you die and during your funeral. Other than that you are always blessed in groups. Communion is with everyone, marriage is two people; yet here he was, giving me my own blessing in front of the still growing crowd.

He prayed to God for me. And not in that "I'll pray for your soul" way. Father Kenny gave me a real blessing out loud and in front of everyone present. And he said, "God protect her and her gifts".

I waited over thirty years for this confirmation.

Chapter 11 ½

A LETTER FROM KAIDEN'S MOM

Dear Terry,

How do I thank you enough for not only sharing your gift with me, but for bringing so much peace into my life? I'm beyond grateful to have met you.

After losing my son in 2013 I was left lost and confused. I believed the darkness would eventually consume my mind with all the "what if's". But because of your beautiful gifts, I was able to know all my heart needed in order to heal. You've helped me grow in so many ways since our first encounter. So to simply say thank you could never be enough. You are a wonderful, kind, and loving person and I am blessed to have witnessed your greatness.

Forever Grateful.

P.S. You told me Kaiden plays with a red and white balloon in my son's room. My son turned one in November. I got him a bunch of balloons. It's now May and the red and white balloon is the only one still floating.

You are incredible.

Chapter 12

MY THEORY OF HELL

Like the word soulmate, I've also searched for the meaning of hell in dictionaries. Dictionary results varied. One stated Hell was a place in various religions thought to be a spiritual realm of evil and suffering. It's traditionally depicted as a place of perpetual fire beneath the earth where the wicked are punished after death. Really? Sounds like Earth to me!

Being spiritual, or having spirituality, refers to a broad set of principles that transcend all religions. Spirituality is about the relationship between ourselves and something larger. Mind, Body, and Soul are all necessary components if one is to attain the state of spirituality. With that said, I believe that hell, as well as heaven, resides deep within our souls.

I believe when we pass we must endure a life review. I use the word endure because it's certainly a physical feat. All of our primary senses are involved in the review process; sight, scent, touch, taste and sound. Depending on the soul the review can be unpleasant.

During the life review, we see what we once did to others. We hear the words that were expressed during pleasant exchanges or elicited exchanges that caused hurt feelings. Everything has an energy vibration; your words, thoughts, and deeds.

Some vibrations have a scent attached to them. Our sense of smell is vivid and heightened during the life review which may or may not be a good thing. Ask any pregnant woman. A heightened sense of smell can be crippling. With smell can also come the taste of contentment or bitterness.

The primary sense of touch is expressed exclusively through feeling. Since we don't take our earthly bodies to heaven, we must feel what our actions and words made the other person feel like. For example, let's say we went out of our way to make an individual or animal feel better since all creatures have souls. We may have smiled at a stranger we didn't know was having a bad day. We may have picked up a turtle that was trying to cross a dangerous road. Or we watered a dying flower or sat in silence with a friend who's grieving. During your life review all of your actions are felt by the other person's point of view. Therein lies the rub. The touch. The pleasure or pain that we created. Pain creates heavy energy.

If the majority of our actions allowed us to feel good about ourselves, and we were humbled by those actions that had a heavier energy surrounding them, then it will be easier for us to accept ourselves, move toward the light and enjoy our just rewards. However, if we led a life full of hatred and misdeeds, then we doom ourselves to a "hell-like" existence. Fear can consume us. So can a lack of self-worthiness or just the opposite can happen.

Our ego can tell us we're better than what we experienced. It makes us feel our God light has it wrong. We are the victim instead of the perpetrator of our own misdeeds. We forget that we all came from the light and it is into the light we can return.

I was born Roman Catholic. We Catholics believe that if we tell God we're sorry for our misdeeds, all is forgiven. But it really doesn't work like that. Saying you're sorry and feeling that sorrow are two very different things. It's easy to say, 'God, I'm sorry that I didn't go to church today.' Words only convey a verbal communication between you and your Higher Being.

Let's say you were watching a movie about the crucifixion of Jesus and during the movie a particular moment actually made something stir within you. You might have felt sorrow, humiliation or regret for not giving your Higher Being the love and respect you now feel He or She deserves by not going to church. That is the moment of truly being sorry. The ironic part is that you were already forgiven before you felt this humbling. It will be harder for you to forgive yourself than it was to be forgiven by your Higher Being.

Let's take this concept away from religion. Let's say you were a bully in school. You might have been a bully due to a lack of self-confidence or a need to be accepted by the cool kids. There was an unfortunate classmate that became the victim of this pack mentality and during the school years, you consistently aided in the efforts to make this kid's life miserable. After maturing and having a child of your own in the school system, there is now a bully bothering your child. You know how the parents of that child feel and how your own bullying victim must have felt. Not a good feeling.

Let's take this a step further. You find out that your old classmate lives and shops in your town. Do you go out of your way to avoid him because you're embarrassed about your past actions (hell) or do you welcome the chance to make things right?

We actually condemn ourselves to an afterlife, or hell, because we're experiencing such heavy feelings. We feel that we don't trust the light, aren't worthy of the light, or just want to keep the control and not face the unknown.

You're going to think I'm crazy, but I truly believe deep down inside we are all worthy of the light.

Chapter 12 ½

DANIELLE'S READING

Theresa: I'm being told to mention the month of March.

Danielle: That's my husband's birthday.

Theresa: I have his grandfather coming in and he is telling me that a boy will be coming into the family.

Danielle: Maybe I'll be getting pregnant.

Theresa: He's telling me that he would like to have this child have his name as the child's middle name.

Danielle: His name is ███████████.

Theresa: He is mentioning Nick. Who is Nick?

Danielle: Another grandchild's name.

Theresa: The grandfather is just using a family name as one of his confirmations. I'm now seeing the month of September, so either the month itself means something to you, the ninth of any month or the name

Michael or Michelle because this is Archangel Michael's month.

Danielle: Yes, it's the name Michelle. She was my cousin's cousins. She died ten years ago.

Theresa: She does make me feel that she is still being mentioned within her family.

Danielle: Yes. All the time.

Theresa: She has a funny sense of humor. She says she comes to whoever mentions her name because she doesn't want to be talked about behind her back. She smiles when she says that.

Danielle: Yes, it sounds like something she would say.

Theresa: She makes me feel she had a hand in her passing.

Danielle: Yes.

Theresa: She wants you to know that she has found peace.

Danielle: Good.

Theresa: She told me that she is in charge of rabbits over there. Do you know why?

Danielle: That's so funny you should say that. She and my cousin always had rabbit keychains.

Theresa: Maybe she's in charge of them there because she used to walk around with one of their paws! Just kidding. But nothing is a coincidence so I bet you'll start to see more rabbits cross your path. Who is Christine or Tina?

Danielle: My cousins had a friend named Christine. Why?

Theresa: Michelle wants you to tell your cousin to tell Christine that she needs to hold on a little longer. Michelle isn't showing me the reason behind the message, but wants to make sure Christine receives the message.

Danielle: Okay.

Theresa: You picked the August colored pencil in the box. Since there is no such thing as a coincidence, what does August mean to you?

Danielle: That's my Godson's birthday.

Theresa: How old is he?

Danielle: Five years old.

Theresa: They want you to know they will want to label him in school.

Danielle: That just happened.

Theresa: They say he doesn't deserve the label and to fight it.

Danielle: His parents are doing that currently.

Theresa: Good. I now have an older gentleman coming in. He's making my throat hurt. Who had the tube down his throat?

Danielle: I don't know.

Theresa: I'm in the grandfather tier.

Danielle: I have two grandfathers there. Which one?

Theresa: He says he comes through the person that knows the Carmine/Carmen or Carmela.

Danielle: ███████████ was my grandmother's friend.

Theresa: Okay. Who does this grandmother belong to?

Danielle: My mother.

Theresa: Then it's your mother's father.

Danielle: Oh my God! He never comes through.

Theresa: He is telling me to tell you that you did good.

Danielle: With?

Theresa: Choosing a new house. Was there a choice between two houses?

Danielle: Yes, but I don't know if I picked the right one.

Theresa: You did. The house will need a little work though.

Danielle: It does.

Theresa: Your grandfather also wants you to know that you will not be raising your children there.

Danielle: Good! My heart wasn't in it.

Theresa: He knows. It'll be easier for you to fix it and sell it. You would not have been able to do that with the other house. Who is Anne Marie or Maryanne?

Danielle: I know a couple. My mother-in-law or my husband's grandmother. Both their names were Maryanne.

Theresa: No. I'm not feeling it.

Danielle: Hmm. Oh wait! My grandmother's name is ███████████ Marie!

Theresa: Is she passed?

Danielle: No, but her husband, my grandfather, is. He's the grandfather that came in earlier.

Theresa: Okay. I can go there then. We just came full circle. Is this grandmother having knee or hip problems?

Danielle: Yes.

Theresa: Okay. They're just confirming the energy of your grandmother. They want to tell you Vinny is with them. Who was Vincent?

Danielle: Actually, I had an Aunt Vinnie.

Theresa: Oh sorry. She wants to say hello.

Danielle: Oh good.

Theresa: They want you to know that they were at a babies hospital recently.

Danielle: My daughter was in a babies hospital recently.

Theresa: They want you to know they were at the hospital prior to your arrival. Grandpa Ed is showing me property with overgrown grass. It drives him nuts.

Danielle: That has to be my property. We actually moved into his house. It was such a mess inside and outside.

Theresa: Well please make the outside appealing as well he says so you can make money and get the house you will stay in. Where is the full-length mirror?

Danielle: In the garage.

Theresa: They are telling me to ask you to move it. They use that mirror as a portal and are tired of coming in through the garage.

Danielle: Oh God.

Theresa: Don't worry. It's only your loved ones using that mirror. How do you know ███████████?

Danielle: That's my husband's best friend.

Theresa: There was a blessing trying to get to him, but he's blocking the positive energy. He isn't aware that he's doing it. I have a friend of your husband's coming in. He wants you to know he doesn't come in the house too often, but when he does he sees your husband pretending to watch T.V. but your husband is actually thinking about him.

Danielle: Yes, his friend just passed. My husband does sit in front of the TV and looks distant.

Theresa: He wants me to tell you that he only visits those who loved him. He makes me feel that not everyone had the heart he did, so he chooses to visit only those with the same type of heart. He also wants you to know that he didn't mean to freak your daughter out. Did she wake up really crying one night out of the blue?

Danielle: Just the other night. She was sleeping and screaming. We ran into her room and her eyes were still closed but she was screaming and rigid.

Theresa: Yea. He said she was freaking out and that he is sorry. He couldn't meet her when he was alive. Is that right?

Danielle: Yes. My husband wanted to wait until he was on the right path.

Theresa: He calls her a sleeping angel. She has the blue light around her which is a very powerful light. He tells me your daughter was supposed to pass during your pregnancy. Does this make any sense to you?

Danielle: Yes. I fell during the pregnancy and went into early labor.

Theresa: He wants you to know that not only Archangel Michael watches over her, but the Virgin Mother herself. So does she have a middle name of Mary or Maria?

Danielle: No, but it's funny. My daughter goes over to the statue of Mary that I have and kisses Her and talks to Her. She had the flu recently and I thought she was delirious because she kept telling me that the Lady is there and just the other day she told me she was talking to the Lady.

Theresa: Your friend just lit up his unfiltered cigarette. He had to be a chain smoker because he's getting ready to light another one. He has some nerve coming into my kitchen and smoking without permission!

Danielle: (Laughing)

Theresa: He wants to confirm the age of thirty-three. Who is around that age?

Danielle: My husband.

Theresa: He tells me he won't just drop by anymore. He wanted to check up on his friend, but mostly he was curious about your daughter. He has since learned that you can't just visit someone because you're curious. There has to be a higher purpose for the visit. Your grandfather wants you to know that there is water under the ground in the yard.

Danielle: Okay.

Theresa: He is also showing me a cake. Whose birthday or anniversary is coming up soon or just passed?

Danielle: It was just my anniversary.

Theresa: Your grandmother is bringing in Margie, Margaret or Peggy.

Danielle: That's my grandmother's cousin. We do mention her.

Theresa: Your grandmother wants you to know that she travels with company. Not because anything bad is going to happen, but she wants you to check your smoke alarm.

Danielle: Oh my god! It keeps going off and I am freaked out about it.

Theresa: Just change the battery. Your grandmother is handing you black olives, not green olives. Why?

Danielle: I love black olives, not green olives.

Theresa: Okay. So she's showing me a confirmation by telling me which olives you prefer. Your grandmother confirms that you will not have privacy in your house.

Danielle: Yes! I was just saying that.

Theresa: Your grandmother wants you to tell me about the puppy story.

Danielle: The puppy story?

Theresa: Yes. What is she trying to tell me?

Danielle: Oh wow. I can't believe this. No one knows this story. Every night I tell a story I made up about a puppy named Cody to my daughter. I started telling this story to my daughter since she was two months old. I used to have a puppy named Cody and this dog used to stay with my grandmother every day.

Theresa: Your grandmother wants you to know that she hears you tell that story every night. She not only brings your dog Cody every night to hear this story, but she tells me that you have a stuffed animal that looks like Cody.

Danielle: I do! It's in my daughter's bed.

Theresa: Your grandmother shows me your daughter using both hands. She will continue to not have a dominant hand for the rest of her life.

Danielle: Yea. We still can't tell if she will be right or left handed.

Theresa: She will be both. Your grandmother wants me to mention Mondays to you. Why?

Danielle: Because that is the only night of the week that I do not put my daughter to sleep. I work late Monday nights.

Theresa: Your grandmother tells you not to worry about Monday nights. She watches over your daughter on those nights. Your grandmother wants you to know that the energy in your daughter's legs is off. Grandma also makes me feel a little numbness in that area as well.

Danielle: She has started walking on her tippy toes and complains a little about her legs.

Theresa: Okay. If they mention a particular area of the body that part of the body will mend whether by time or doctor intervention. Keep in mind that your grandmother is not putting the feeling of dread around this problem. Who is Jane/Janice? Alive, not passed.

Danielle: My mother's best friend.

Theresa: Is her dad on the other side?

Danielle: Yes.

Theresa: He is coming through asking you to please tell his daughter he's okay and that he trusts her to make the right decision.

Danielle: That makes sense.

Theresa: I hate common names. But when they insist, I will deliver the name. They also want to reach out to Joe. Who is Joe?

Danielle: My husband.

Chapter 13

A NOTE FROM THE AUTHOR

My name is Heather. I crossed paths with Theresa years ago. Fate chose me to be her writer for this book and I have had the pleasure of climbing inside her head for the last few years. Being friends with a medium is awesome. I tell Theresa very little about myself on purpose in order to be amazed when little tidbits of information trickle through during a work meeting or lunch date. Sometimes the messages aren't even for me.

One day, Theresa and I scheduled an outdoor meeting, on a beautiful day, to discuss the writing of this book. I chose my local riverfront even further upstate from what Theresa considered the "country". I chose the spot for several reasons. For one, I'm Pagan - a blanket term I use to give a "name" to my personal beliefs since people seem to need a name. That day my gut told me it was best to meet surrounded by Mother Nature.

The riverfront in my hometown is beautiful. You can see so many mountain ranges from one spot. The town had carved out pathways and added sculptures and benches, built docks and boat launches. My father had taken me to the riverfront a few days prior and I figured it was the perfect place for our next meeting. Plus it was easy-on, easy-off the highway and Theresa could get lost driving straight.

Her instructions were to get off the highway, go over the tracks and make an immediate right. Then go to the end and park. After a brief Hello I turned down her offer for a chair three times, helped her carry a few things, and we made our way to a secluded shady spot under a big tree overlooking the river. She sat down on her chair. I sat down on the grass and attempted to get down to business. That's when she hit me with a "Who's John?".

"I know a few of them," I replied. Who doesn't know at least two Johns?

Without missing a beat she returned with, "The last one you saw in public".

Okay. Now I am zoned in on the last John I interacted with in public. It was a John from my childhood I saw just the day before. I hadn't bumped into him for years until we both ended up inside the same gas station. This was no coincidence. "Got it. What about him?"

"His father is here. He's here a lot. I don't know why, but he likes it down here."

Theresa went on to give me a message for John. Afterward, I told her why he was here. John's father was a fireman whose life was taken on 9/11; the day terrorist crashed planes into two New York skyscrapers known as the Twin Towers.

Had Theresa made the left when she first arrived and drove towards the train station, parked and walked to the waterfront, she would have seen the monument they put there in his memory. It's surrounded by flowers and bushes. A nice spot for a quiet reflection. But she didn't drive that way. She had made the right and had no idea his small tribute on the other side of the park even existed.

I ended up bumping into John shortly after this day at that very same gas station. I was sitting in my car ready to leave when I saw a red truck park itself three spots over. Johnny hopped out of the truck and went inside. He hadn't noticed me so I could have just kept going, but I couldn't leave. I had a message for John and a pull to give it to him. But I hadn't really spoken to him in years and felt extremely awkward approaching him with a message. I now understood what Theresa meant about fighting through your ego. She'd also told me to ask for signs, so instead of going inside, I asked for a sign telepathically.

If I'm supposed to give him this message he'll come out of the store so I don't have to do in front of other people.

A few seconds later he walked out to his truck, and threw his door open to look for his wallet. I thought about that for a moment. It wasn't like he came out because he was finished. He just so happen to have left his wallet in the car by mistake. That was my sign. So I got out my door and approached him. I opened with, "So I'm writing this book for a medium and I have a message for you that came out during a work meeting."

I gave the message. Turns out John had been spending a lot of time down at the river lately. He had something going on in his life and was spending his alone time near his father's memorial. I was able to give him the clarity that his father was with him and heard his prayers.

Now back to my meeting with Theresa that day at the riverfront. After "who's John," came "Who's Frank? Or Frankie?"

"I know two," I replied.

"The one whose stomach you're always worried about. Wow! You worry about his stomach a lot. He's fine. He may get sick but he'll be fine."

She was talking about my new kitten, Frankincense, Frankie for short. When my cousin found him on the side of the road he was only a few weeks old and looked like he'd swallowed a tennis ball. I adopted him shortly after and had already taken him to the vet twice to figure out what was causing it. He is fine and much older now. Turns out his breed is a bit glutinous meaning Frankie's most likely going to end up on diet food later in life. She was right. I needn't have worried myself sick that Frankie had a tumor. Everything was fine. This is what it's like being friends with a medium.

Another meeting, this one at a diner. We walked in and were seated right away. She gave me the Italian kiss kiss on each cheek and threw her palms up. "What's with the fox?"

At this point I knew only one thing, she said fox and that's my husband's spirit animal. "Not mine but what about it?"

Theresa has only been to my home once right after we moved in and everything was still in boxes.

"The red one. It's high on a shelf," she raised her hand in the air to emphasis. "It's separated from the rest of the house and wherever it is has great energy. Who's fox is it?"

"It's Maks' (my husband). I keep it behind glass in the cabinet where I showcased the tree sculptures I make."

Then she went on to give me a message for Maks'. This is what it's like to be friends with a medium. It's a Saturday morning phone call from her to say, "you know that dream you had where you were being haunted by something that had green eyes?" Know it. I just woke up from that dream.

But to date, my absolute most favorite Theresa story is what happened between her and my cousin that rescued my kitten, Jayme. A few years prior something very sad happened in Jayme's life and I wanted to take her for a reading. Theresa's a busy woman, so I brought Jayme to a business meeting for the making of this book. Theresa and I would get to business then Jayme was going to be read. At least that's how it was supposed to happen. But Spirit does as it wishes and in the middle of discussing chapter two Theresa exclaimed, "Oh here's a new sign. I've never seen this one before!"

Theresa and I had been discussing what types of signs she saw as all of our signs are different. What means something to her may mean something else to me. I watched her draw a grid. "They make me feel ownership. Who's Makalah. I almost feel home ownership but the grid is new. Perhaps it's an apartment building."

Jayme smiled. "I live in an apartment and have a friend named Makalah."

Theresa continued. "So this is for you. She came into your life during a lot of sorrow. She was there for you for something. There's a baby but something's wrong. He has weak legs, his hands and feet - something is wrong with them, (She pulled her hands into fists to demonstrate.) Something is wrong with his forehead. I don't know if it's distended…"

At this point both Jayme and I were in tears. She swears I started it. Jayme lost a son a few years ago. He had stopped growing in the womb and it was discovered he had triploidy - a rare genetic condition where the body has an extra set of chromosomes. Jayme would later tell me Theresa was extremely accurate when naming the symptoms. Makalah had also lost a child and was Jayme's support system when she made the difficult decision to be induced rather than terminate. She was able to hold him, but he had passed while she was in labor.

"Why do you think you won't have more kids?"

"It's been my biggest fear since."

"How come you don't read anymore," Theresa asked.

"I just haven't since he passed."

"And what's with the bananas?"

"That's funny. I don't really like fruits and vegetables, but when I was pregnant all I wanted was bananas."

"I see children," Theresa continued. "But you have to better yourself. Read again. Get back into doing the things you like to do. Eat healthy. Stop that unhealthy stuff your doing. I don't know what it is because they're showing me a black curtain. It's none of my business. When you step off this chair, it's your choice to step in the right direction. But he's not coming back. He can't come back."

I'm a believer in reincarnation. I had a heart to heart with Jayme after the baby passed. I told her I believe you are reincarnated over and over again until you learn your lessons and lead a good life as a good person. Then you don't have to come back but you can choose to come back to help other people. Those are the people you'd swear were walking angels in human form. They're the ones that cross your path with messages to help you on your way. I told Jayme that I believe when I child passes so suddenly it's because they only had one last thing they had to do in order to reach that level of Spirit. Then they too become walking angels as they have finally reached Nirvana. But this was a private conversation we had between just her and I.

Theresa smacked her knee and shouted, "Holy shit! I can't believe it! I've never seen this before! He can't come back because he was never meant to be in human form. He was your guardian angel. That's why he couldn't be in human form. A human body could never hold him. Your guardian angel said he took human form to save you and you already know why."

Jayme had been in a long-term toxic relationship when she got pregnant. I won't go into details about what went on while she was in the hospital, but let's just say it gave her the strength she needed to finally leave him for good. Shortly after she met a man that treats her like a queen. They have a son together who is one hundred percent healthy. He celebrates his first birthday soon.

Watching Jayme receive these messages from Theresa that day was amazing. I was so glad I went with my gut and brought her with me that day. It would be the first and only time I brought someone to a meeting other than my mother.

It was truly an honor to be chosen to write this book for my dear friend and mentor Theresa Marotta. Without her, I may never have found my true path. And for that, I am forever grateful.

Theresa taught me to open my eyes and head forth with no fear. Why does it matter what religion you are? Or how you pray? Truth is, it doesn't. Just believe. Believe in yourself. Believe in love. Believe in the light and you will never be truly alone so there's no reason to ever be afraid.

Sincerely,

Heather T. Stone
Theresa's "Ghost" Writer

Chapter 13 ½

A LETTER FROM TIMOTHY'S MOM

Hi Theresa!

When I came to you for a reading you told me, "Your father wants you to know your son is going to get sick and go in the hospital. The doctors aren't going to know exactly what's wrong with him. He's going to undergo a lot of tests, but he's going to be fine in the end." You also told me my father wanted me to know he's going to be with me and doesn't want me to panic.

I'm thinking to myself, what the heck?! But okay, good to know! Having worked in the Emergency Department for several years that seemed confusing to me. How are the doctors going to know what tests to run if they don't know what's wrong with him? Like everything you've ever told me, I remember it and tuck it away because I never know if what you tell me is going to happen the next day, week, month or year, but I always remember it.

About ten months later I was at work in the mailroom one morning and I find a handful of silver coins on the floor in a cluster. The day I first met you, after a family reading, you told me my father is going to leave me silver coins. I find them in the most random places now too. How strange was it to find a handful of coins in a busy place; right there on the floor. It was so profound that I took a picture of them, texted it to my sister and said, "Dad says hi".

It was later that day I got a call from my son's school nurse saying he had a headache and blurry vision. He had a dose of medication and, since it was the end of the school day, he was continuing on with his after school activities. His martial arts school picks him up from middle school. I called the martial arts school to advise them he wasn't feeling well and may not be able to participate in class.

Later, I called and spoke to one of the instructors to ask how he was doing. The instructor replied, "He looks TERRIBLE!!" Worried, I told the instructor I was going to leave work and pick him up. When I arrived, my son wasn't able to walk to the car himself. The instructors had to carry him out. One of the instructors asked if I was taking him to the hospital. Take him to the hospital for what? He has a headache. I'm taking him home to rest and give him more medication. Then all of a sudden the reading pops into my head. Is this it? Is this not it? Is this it? Is this not it? I'm going back and forth in my head trying to figure out what's going with him and IS THIS IT??

I thank everyone for looking after him and helping get him in the car and we head home. I'm asking him what hurts? When did you start not feeling well? Is it your stomach? Do you feel like you have the flu? My son's reply back to me was, "No. I don't want pizza for dinner."

I said, "Okay. We're going to the hospital now." I made a u-turn in the middle of the road and went to the Emergency Department.

We pull up and thank goodness there were friends and people I knew from when I worked there currently working. They had to take him out of the car in a wheelchair and put him right in a room. I explain his symptoms; headache and his altered mental status. They immediately think he tried some drug or was drugged somehow at school; whether it was accidental in a science lab or someone put something in his drink at lunch. I called my husband, a police officer and a nurse, and told him, "I don't care where you're going or what you're doing right now. You have to come to the hospital because there's something going on with our son." I call my mother and sister to tell them we're in the ER to keep them in the loop too.

The doctor evaluates him and my poor child can barely verbalize anything. He didn't know my name, but knew I was his mother. He didn't know his school's name, the street he lived on or anything else. He wasn't able to follow directions to lay down or squeeze the doctor's hands. Now he starts vomiting. It was heartbreaking to see in front of my eyes.

The urine tox screening comes back negative so it's not drugs. Now they think maybe concussion, Lyme or Meningitis. In the meantime they do a head CT (Cat Scan) and that's negative. They also want to do a spinal tap now and are talking about transferring him to another hospital where there are specialists. Parts of the reading are echoing in my head.

"The doctors aren't going to know what's wrong with him. He's going to undergo a lot of tests. He's going to be okay. Don't panic."

Every time I was going to panic, I would hear in my head. "He's going to be okay. Don't panic." I lean over to him in the bed and tell him, "You may not understand me right now, but I know you're going to be okay and you'll get through this". He looked so scared like he didn't know what was going on, but I kept telling him, "I know you're going to be okay," while smiling confidently and remembering, "He's going to be okay. Don't panic".

The doctor asks me if I'm okay and if I need to sit down. I say I'm fine, thank you. I guess he's used to parents freaking out at this point. I calmly ask how's he going to be transferred? By ground or by air? Who's the accepting doctor? He said he'd get the doctor's name and be right back.

My mother, sister and the rest of my Italian family are planning to meet us at the other hospital. The doctor returns and advises he's being transferred by ground because of the poor weather conditions outside. He gives us the accepting doctor's name. This is now eight hours since the nurse's phone call and my son's being transferred to another hospital. By the time we arrive at the other hospital some cognitive functions and memory returned. It's a miracle my son has turned the corner and is now slightly better than what he's been.

My whole family has taken over the waiting room. I go tell them he seems to be getting better very slowly. My sister looks at me and asks, "How are you so calm through all of this and not freaking out?" I told her I prayed he'd be okay and he is, not mentioning the reading yet.

It was determined by the specialists he had a hemiplegic, or complex, migraine that presents with stroke like symptoms and can be scary especially in a young child. He was eventually discharged a few hours later after more observation and recovery time. He went home walking and talking, explaining his views of things. How he wanted to answer the doctor's questions, but couldn't remember the right words to use in the sentence or the words just came out wrong. He remembers wanting to try to write down his answers, but didn't know how to ask for a pen and paper. He meant to call out for the doctor, but couldn't remember that word so he used the word "nurse" instead. It was in the car ride on the way home I told him we had an angel watching over us today.

I am so grateful for the reading you gave me that day because it changed my whole perspective on the situation and, yes, although still upsetting, I didn't panic at all and I knew he was going to be okay.

Gratefully Yours

Chapter 13 3/4

INDEX OF THERESA'S SIGNS

I would like to emphasis, once again, that although I am about to provide a list of sign meanings mentioned in the book, these are MY signs. Your signs will and should be different as we are each unique personalities with unique perspectives.

Touch: If I feel = it means:
- Right breast pain = Breast cancer
- Middle chest pain = Anxiety
- Head pain = Head trauma or illness
- Dizziness = Psychic abilities because I react to the change in energy
- Feet pain = Feet problems or diabetes
- Right side of my nose running = Drug abuse
- Left side of my nose running = Alcohol abuse
- Severe pain with burning = Gunshot or stabbing
- Throat closing up = Tubes down the throat or choking
- Instant nausea and dizziness = Heavy spirit

Sight - Images / Hearing - Spoken words:
If I see = what it means to me
- Eruptions = Coming together / new life
- Uniform = Wears a uniform to work like a police person, fire person, security guard

- Horse = Someone owns or rides horses, or they have a connection to Bronx, New York
- An image of a pot being stirred / Stirring the pot = Someone is starting trouble or someone is a troublemaker
- Swan = The actual animal or swans mate for life

What My Months Mean to Me:

January:
January / 1st of any month / the number 1
Either the month itself means something, the 1st of any month means something, or the number one means something. I can be given the sign by either hearing the word January or seeing the birthstone for January. These types of signs appear for each month.

February:
February / 2nd of any month / the number 2

March:
March / 3rd of any month / the number 3

The names Joseph, Josephine, Joey. Saint Joseph's name day is in March and he's the patron Saint of moving and houses. It could mean someone is moving.

April:
April / the 4th of any month / the number 4

May:
May / the 5th of any month / the number 5
The names Mary and Maria. May is the month of Our Lady the Virgin Mary in the Catholic religion.

June:
June / the 6th of any month / the number 6
The name Anthony. June is Saint Anthony's month.
He was one of two miracle workers. This could mean
someone has been praying a lot for a miracle.

July:
July / the 7th of any month / the number 7
The names Carmela or Carmine. July is Our Lady of
Mount Carmel's month.

August:
August / the 8th of any month / the number 8

September:
September / the 9th of any month / the number 9
The name Michael or Michelle. September is
Archangel Michael's month. Someone is a police
person or fire person.

October:
October / the 10th of any month / the number 10
The name Theresa or Terry. October is Saint
Teresa's month. Or someone lived/lives near a
church.

November:
November / the 11th of any month / the number 11

December:
December / the 12th of any month / or the number 12
The names Lucy or Lucille. December is Saint Lucy's
month. Saint Lucy is the Saint you pray to for eyes. It
could mean someone has eye problems.

I learn new signs every day. Should you choose to nurture your gifts and begin to read signs, in time you'll figure out what your own signs are and what they mean to you. Keep an open mind and always remember...

It's only a matter of perspective...

Made in the USA
Middletown, DE
22 September 2021

48786540R00163